Making the Workplace a Worthplace

Marvin Karlins

Professor of Management
University of South Florida

KENDALL/HUNT PUBLISHING COMPANY
2460 Kerper Boulevard P.O. Box 539 Dubuque, Iowa 52004-0539

To Arnold . . . who set the standards by which all fathers are judged.

ABOUT THE AUTHOR

Marvin Karlins, Professor of Management, received his B.A. degree from the University of Minnesota (*Summa Cum Laude* and Phi Beta Kappa) and his Ph.D. in psychology from Princeton University. He has taught at Princeton, the City University of New York and the University of South Florida where he has twice been recognized as the outstanding teacher of the year in the School of Business. He is the author of fifteen books and a frequent contributor to professional and popular journals. Dr. Karlins also serves as a consultant to numerous organizations both in the United States and abroad.

CONTENTS

CONTENTS

PREFACE

This book is about management and how you can become a better manager. It is also a book about psychology and how you can use it to modify behavior in a positive manner. And, finally, it is a book that provides a blueprint for changing the workplace into a worthplace, a place where personal *and* economic growth can coexist. Some portions of this text appeared originally in my book *The Human Use of Human Resources*, published in 1981 by McGraw-Hill.

A manager's job isn't easy. If 25 years as a consultant, psychologist and professor of business has taught me anything, it is a profound sense of respect for the men and women who choose management as a career. Theirs is often a thankless job requiring unwavering dedication and boundless energy to deal with seemingly endless problems and crises. Yet, it is also an occupation of crucial importance, where a person can make a difference in the world. Management, in short, is "where the action is" . . . and that's where you probably want to be.

Although a manager's job is difficult, it can be mastered, and mastered well. The purpose of this book is to make you a better manager by showing you how to use human resources both effectively and humanely.

The first section of the text, "A Theoretical Orientation," will provide you with the philosophical and conceptual basis for human resource management. How to actually manage those resources effectively will be discussed in Section Two, "Theory Goes to Work." It is here that I will be teaching you the skills necessary to function successfully in the workplace—skills that can be learned, and have been, by thousands of individuals just like yourself. Finally, Section Three lets "You Be the Manager" . . . applying what you've learned in a series of exercises and cases designed to enhance your personal growth while sharpening your managerial interest and skills.

There are today a growing number of individuals and corporations dedicated to making the job environment a better place to work. I salute their efforts. Yet, there is still a long way to go in the struggle to make the workplace a worthplace. Being a manager in our changing world is a challenging mixture of opportunity and responsibility. I hope the information in this book will help make work more rewarding to both you and those you manage, and hasten the day when all labor and management can work together in a productive and personally satisfying manner.

Marvin Karlins

ACKNOWLEDGMENTS

I would like to recognize with gratitude the contributions of my undergraduate students to this effort. All 50,000 +of you! Thanks for making my teaching experience a learning experience.

"The number one survival skill for today's business manager is the human relations skill—the ability to understand human behavior and to deal with it intelligently."

Karl Albrecht

SECTION ONE

A Theoretical Orientation

A Story with a Moral

$$\boxed{1}$$

"I will pay more for the ability to deal with people than any other ability under the sun."

John D. Rockefeller

A patient is dying. For 13 years the vital signs have deteriorated—a profile of life ebbing inexorably toward oblivion. Everyone familiar with the case is frustrated; intensive examinations and treatments have done little to alleviate the condition. With time running out, a specialist is called in to save the patient where others have failed. He is advised that the patient is in need of major surgery "to remove the malfunctioning organs and replace them with new ones."

The specialist doesn't agree. He believes that the organs can function effectively without surgery if properly treated. He's right. Three years later the patient's vital signs have clearly improved, and the patient is growing at a healthy, robust rate.

Would it surprise you to find out the patient was a *corporation* and the specialist a *manager*? You most likely know the patient: Avis Rent-A-Car. And the specialist? None other than Robert Townsend, the peppery chief executive who engineered Avis's recovery and wrote about it in his irreverent best-seller *Up the Organization*.[1]

When Townsend took command of Avis in 1962 the floundering company hadn't turned a profit in 13 years of life. The rest is corporate history. In 3 years Avis had more than doubled its sales (from $30 million to $75 million) and amassed earnings in excess of $9 million.

How did Townsend do it? With some unorthodox philosophy, hard work, and a deep, abiding faith in his employees. Claims Townsend:

> When I became head of Avis, I was assured that no one at headquarters was any good, and that my first job was to start recruiting a whole new team. Three years later, Hal Geneen, the President of ITT (which had just acquired Avis), after meeting everybody and listening to them in action for a day, said, "I've never seen such depth of management; why, I've already spotted three chief executive officers!" You guessed it. Same people. I'd brought in only two new people, a lawyer and an accountant.[2]

There was nothing wrong with the "internal organs" of Avis's corporate body—and Townsend knew it. Rather than "cutting out" the people he had, he worked with them, provided them with a corporate environment that satisfied their needs, and encouraged them to be productive. And he succeeded.

1. Robert Townsend, *Up the Organization*, Fawcett-Crest, New York, 1970.
2. Ibid., p. 123.

There is a profound lesson to be learned from the story of Robert Townsend. It is this: Success or failure in the business world often turns on a manager's ability to utilize human resources effectively (see Box 1.1). Townsend had that ability, and he used it to turn Avis around. When it came to human resource management, Townsend tried harder. He fully understood the need for motivating workers and made the effort to fire them up at work rather than fire them out of work.

Box 1.1
Let Them Eat Pie

History books are bulging with examples of businesses—large and small—which faltered or failed because of poor human resource management. One of the more spectacular examples involved the bankrupt W. T. Grant Company. The executives of this organization didn't have a monopoly on poor human resource practices; but they went a long way toward establishing a base line against which inappropriate management practices can be measured.

Take, for example, the Company's "negative incentives" program. This human resource nightmare was targeted at store managers who didn't meet their quotas. Their penalties? Some had their ties snipped in half; others were forced to run backward through their stores or push peanuts with their noses. It was rumored (but unconfirmed) that one district manager had to stroll through a hotel lobby in a diaper! Other managers faced the ultimate indignity of being hit in the face with a custard pie.

Let us hope that we have seen the last of these managerial practices in the business world and that the W. T. Grant experience will be a kind of "custard's last stand."

Just How Important Are Human Resources in the Contemporary Economy?

Vitally important. Just *how* vital we are only now beginning to appreciate. Unfortunately, early American managers tended to focus most of their energy and attention on developing the production side of management, ignoring or downplaying the human dimension in the workplace. This bias was understandable considering the temper and knowledge of the times. In the first place, "people resources" were plentiful and easily exploitable (rights of labor were yet to realized). The early managers tended to treat workers much as the early pioneers tended to treat the natural resources on the frontier: as unlimited, cheap, and always replaceable. Conservation of resources just didn't seem relevant in an environment where supply overwhelmed demand and management power over the labor force was so absolute. Secondly, there was the problem of *recognizing* the value of human resources. There was no reason for a manager to grasp the dollar-and-cent value of human resources because profit and loss statements didn't include "people costs" in the balance sheets.

In effect, then, the true value of human resources lay hidden—lost in an era of cheap, easily exploitable labor and bookkeeping systems that ignored the impact of human resources in "bottom-line" profit and loss considerations.

How times have changed! Today the effective utilization of human resources is being touted as a major development in maintaining the health of the American economy—a point of view I heartily endorse. Just as our nation has come to understand that the pioneer view of natural resources is no longer viable—that we must now develop a new respect and working plan for our physical environment—so, too, has management come to realize that the early attitudes toward human resources are obsolete and that a new "ecology" of people as a precious commodity must be instituted.

Think of human resource development as a whole new frontier. Unlike production factors, which have been widely explored and developed, human resource development is still largely unexplored and represents a fertile new area for discoveries and progress.

It is imperative that you—a future manager—make the effort necessary to familiarize yourself with this new frontier, so that you may discover how to get the most out of your human resources—how to encourage sustained high levels of productivity at work. This is particularly true today because American business faces foreign challenges unknown in earlier times. If we are to meet successfully the market thrust of other industrialized nations, we must maintain a productive stance at home that will keep us competitive abroad.

Getting the Most Out of Your Human Resources

Once we recognize the importance of human resources for succeeding in the contemporary business world, the next logical question is, "As a manager, how can I get the most out of the human resources under my direction?" Or, simply, "How can I get the most productivity out of my workers?"

The answer to this question will occupy us for the rest of this book. We will be learning to use the motivational techniques developed by behavioral scientists to keep workers productive and satisfied. We will also be exploring some new ways of conceptualizing labor-management relations. Before we do this, however, it will be instructive to observe the average working environment, for it is from the contemporary workplace that our strategy of effective human resource management will evolve.

Getting the Most Out of Your Human Resources

Making Work More
Than a Four-letter Word

2

"Am I worried about going to hell? Why should I be, I already work there five days a week."

Heavy-equipment operator

Victor Ruiz is a musician residing in Tampa, Florida. He is also a polished amateur golfer with a low handicap and a high degree of dedication to the game. How high? Well, consider one of his rounds as detailed in *Sports Illustrated*:

> Ruiz was going quite well after a few holes at the Rocky Point course. Suddenly pain gripped his chest and he doubled over. His partners suggested that he go back to the clubhouse.
>
> "I was playing too good to quit," says Ruiz, "so I hit myself in the gut and the pain went away. I kept on."
>
> The pain came back, but between pars Ruiz slapped at himself some more. He shot 37 on the first nine and was not about to quit. A friend gave him a coke and some Rolaids.
>
> "I began to feel better," Ruiz recalls, "but soon the pain returned again. This time it was in my arm."
>
> He putted for birdies on the last three holes, making one on the 18th green for 74. Then he all but fell down in a faint. He was rushed home and from there to a hospital, where he was given emergency treatment for the heart attack that had been striking him.
>
> The incident taught him a lesson, Ruiz says.
>
> "That pain in my arm," he explains, "was one reason I was hitting my long irons so straight. It made me shorten my swing."[1]

Picot Floyd also lives in Tampa, Florida, where he has held the post of county commissioner. Unfortunately, some of the county employees were not quite as devoted to their work as Mr. Ruiz was to his golf. At one point Mr. Floyd attempted to stir his workers from their lethargy with a little "wake-up reminder" called the "Employee Death Tag." The yellow tag suggested:

> Because of the close resemblance between death and the normal working attitude in some departments, all supervisors should extend a paycheck as the final test to determine if a worker is really deceased or just snoozing. If the employee does not reach for the paycheck, it reasonably may be assumed that death has occurred.

Things aren't always as they appear, however, and Mr. Floyd cautioned the supervisors: "In some cases, the paycheck-reaching instinct is so strongly developed in the worker that a spasmodic clutching reflex may occur. Don't let this fool you."

Talk about differences in behavior! Mr. Ruiz was highly motivated to pursue his golf game; he played willingly with zest. Contrast this kind of dedication and that of Mr. Floyd's Death Tag recipients, who approached work with all the enthusiasm of bears in hibernation.

---

1. Martin Kane, "The Game's the Thing," *Sports Illustrated*, July 24, 1972, pp. 6-7.

Now I am not suggesting that Mr. Floyd's employees throw themselves into their work with reckless abandon—nor, for that matter, do I think Mr. Ruiz should play the links in the midst of a coronary. It would be nice, however, if Commissioner Floyd's yellow-tagged employees could somehow display a bit of Mr. Ruiz's enthusiasm in their work, be a more productive human resource on the job.

Actually the contrasting behaviors of Mr. Ruiz and the Death Tag employees of Mr. Floyd disturbs those of us involved in the business community. With increasing frequency we observe individuals displaying lackluster performance at work. What makes matters worse is that many of these listless employees are active, alert, and performing to the best of their ability *outside* the workplace. It is almost as if these individuals possess two personalities: one for weekends and evenings, the other for working hours. Why should this be? Are avocational pursuits inherently more interesting and motivating than work? Is the workplace devoid of challenge and stimulation?

The sad truth is that for an increasing segment of employees work is becoming a four-letter word (see Box 2.1). More and more, labor is seen as an activity to be endured, not enjoyed—an unpleasant necessity of life to be done as quickly as possible and forgotten equally as quickly.

A Cost We Can't Afford

What is the cost of such attitudes and feeling about work? Tremendous, for *both* the nation's economy and its employees. For the individual worker it means the squandering of one-third of a lifetime in activity which is distasteful and limiting to personal growth. For American business it means all the evils associated with job dissatisfaction: low morale, absenteeism, reduced productivity, and, in extreme cases, sabotage.

It is a well-established fact that unhappy workers (those whose needs are not being met) are less productive workers; they reduce the ability of American business to survive and prosper in the increasingly competitive world marketplace. As past Undersecretary of the Treasury Charles E. Walker bluntly stated: "If we don't get increased productivity in this country, we might as well put up a sign saying 'going out of business.' Our economic survival is at stake."

Are things hopeless?

Certainly not! I am firmly convinced that it is possible to create a work environment that will stimulate employees to perform to the best of their ability, to their fullest work potential. And I believe that it is the job and responsibility of management to take the steps necessary to create such a work environment. I call such a workplace a *worthplace*, and it is in this worthplace that we will have the best chance to develop workers who want to work and gain personal satisfaction from their labors.

What Is a Worthplace?

A worthplace is any job environment designed to encourage both employee productivity and satisfaction in the conduct of labor. To create such an environment, contemporary managers must be sensitive to both "task" concerns ("getting the job done") and "people" concerns ("being aware of, and responsive to, employees' needs"). When such a condition exists, the workplace is transformed into a "worthplace":

1. a place that emphasizes the importance of people in the work equation;
2. a place where employees are valued and encouraged to ''become all they are capable of becoming'' in the organization;
3. a place where managers, as mentors, provide the supportive environment necessary to encourage employees' growth and development;
4. a place where management attempts to maximize morale and productivity in the workforce so the company can compete from a position of strength in the new world economy.

A worthplace. It is the kind of work environment I hope you will want to create and nurture whenever you manage in an organization. In the next chapter we will learn how behavioral science can help us accomplish such an objective.

Box 2.1
Thank God It's Friday

Work might be as American as apple pie, but judging from some current employee attitudes, it certainly isn't as enjoyable.

Humorous cartoons are popular vehicles for portraying the very unfunny condition of contemporary work. For example, judging from the *Frank and Ernest* cartoon included below, do you think the cartoon character will be very enthusiastic about *any* new job?

Consider also the facing "Work Week" sketch. If a picture is worth ten thousand words, this cartoon should tell you a lot about current worker attitudes toward their jobs. In this comic view of labor, the weekend is seen as an oasis, a refuge, a "safe place" where the employee can escape from the miseries of the workplace and store up enough energy to face Blue Monday. Wednesday becomes "hump" day—the day an employee must "get over" to be more than halfway through the workweek. And Friday? It becomes the vestibule to salvation—or as a movie title has suggested: *Thank God It's Friday*.

If you wish to become an *effective* manager, you must learn how to enhance worker satisfaction *and* productivity on the job. This is what skilled human resource management is all about.

FRANK AND ERNEST

Reprinted by permission. © 1978 NEA, Inc.

Box 2-1 Continued.

The Role of Behavioral Science and the Plus-Plus Relationship $\boxed{3}$

As the next generation of managers it will be your responsibility to create the worthplaces where your employees can reach their full potential as workers and as human beings. To fashion such an environment you must become a *human resource director*, a person who can encourage optimal job performance in your subordinates through *effective leadership* (gaining the respect and cooperation of those you direct) and *motivational practices* (practices that encourage employee productivity and satisfy employee needs).

The Importance of Behavioral Science for Making the Workplace a Worthplace

Behavioral science research findings reveal how you can most effectively lead and motivate your employees — how, in short, you can be a successful manager. Combined with on-the-job experience, these findings can help you optimize your human resource skills and become the best manager you are capable of becoming.

And becoming an effective human resource manager is no small accomplishment! As industry consultant Karl Albrecht correctly emphasizes: "The #1 survival skill for today's business manager is the human relations skill — the ability to understand human behavior and to deal with it intelligently."

That's *your* survival Albrecht is talking about. And he's right: A study by Henchey & Company revealed that 76 percent of the executives in its "outplacement" program lost their jobs because of "difficulties in interpersonal relationships." Only 14 percent of the terminations were attributed to failures in job performance.[1]

Playing the Role of Psychologist

It is recognized in Hollywood that the great movie stars are proficient at playing many different kinds of roles. The same can be said for skilled managers. Throughout your career you will be called upon to play different roles, to wear "different hats" in performing your duties. One of those roles is *psychologist*. As Dr. Harry Levinson observes: "We're going to have to go a lot deeper into what makes people tick. Managers will have to know and understand as much about the psychology of motivation as they know about marketing, EDP, and other increasingly functional areas."[2]

---

1. Cited in M. Karlins and E. Hargis, "Science Friction: What Do Managers Have Against Behavioral Science in the Workplace?" Unpub. Manuscript, 1989.
2. Ibid., p. 4.

Now I am *not* suggesting that to be an effective manager you must be trained as a psychologist to direct the activities of others. Nor, for that matter, am I recommending that you have to be a professional accountant to work with a budget or a trained economist to make company forecasts. What I *am* suggesting is that you gain a basic familiarity with some of the concepts of psychology, accounting, economics, and so forth—so that when the need arises on the job, you will have the information necessary to effectively manage the situation.

Harold Leavitt, managerial psychologist, has argued:

> Some kind of psychological theory is just as necessary for the manager dealing with human problems as is electrical and mechanical theory for the engineer dealing with machine problems. Without theory the engineer has no way of diagnosing what might be wrong when the engine stops, no way of preestimating the effects of a proposed change in design. Without some kind of psychological theory, the manager cannot attach meaning to the red flags of human disturbance; nor can he predict the likely effects of changes in organization or personnel policy.[3]

In Section 2 of this book I will be giving you some of the psychological and behavioral science findings Dr. Leavitt believes you will need to deal most effectively with the human problems you are bound to encounter. We will be focusing on those findings that can be *readily applied* on the job to help you manage your human resources with the highest proficiency—in the words of management pioneer Mary Parker Follett, "get things done through other people." For now it is sufficient for you to recognize the importance of behavioral science findings in helping you develop into a humane and effective manager.

The Specter of Behavior Control

A major goal of contemporary psychology is the *control of human behavior*. And, yes, one of *your* major goals as a manager who studies psychological theories and techniques will be to learn how to control more effectively the behavior of your subordinates—to get them to do what you want them to do.

Does this sound sinister? Machiavellian? To many of you it might smack of "1984ism" and be repugnant. Yet let me point out that each of you *already* tries to control the behavior of others. The woman who tries to persuade a friend to carry out some task or the man who spanks his child are practicing rudimentary forms of behavior control—rudimentary in comparison with the more sophisticated, effective behavior control techniques used by individuals trained in psychology or in the use of psychologically based behavioral science techniques. You will be learning in this book how to regulate human behavior in a more systematic, scientific, powerful manner—in short, how to control your human resources more effectively.

There is nothing wrong with attempting to control the behavior of others *as long as it is done in a responsible manner*. I do ask you, however, always to remember the following:

I will be giving you information that will make you a more powerful behavior controller (more proficient in your ability to regulate the actions of your employees). With this increased proficiency comes an increasing obligation to use your behavior-changing power in an ethical, humane way—in a manner which will benefit both the behavior controller and the controllee. That is what I mean when I speak of the human use (should I say *humane* use?) of human resources.

---

3. Ibid., p. 6.

Sometimes we become so accustomed to our behavior-changing power as to forget we possess it and use it in a careless or callous fashion. This is an unforgiveable error. One can never afford to be casual with behavior-changing power.

Remember that to possess behavior-changing power is both a privilege and a burden. Don't use it unless you are willing to do so in a responsible and ethical way that will benefit your employees as well as you.

Establishing the Plus-Plus Relationship

In the spirit of what I have just said, we come to a major concept in the effective *and* ethical use of behavior control on the job: the creation of the ++ (*plus-plus*) relationship. The ++ (also called *win-win*)relationship refers to the establishment of a work environment whereby the needs of management and labor are both fulfilled: specifically, an environment where productivity (management goal) and satisfaction of personal needs (employee goals) coexist (see Figure 3.1).

Condition	Management	Labor	Result
"plus-plus" High job productivity High need satisfaction	+	+	"win-win"
"plus-minus" High job productivity Low need satisfaction	+	–	"win-lose"
"minus-plus" Low job Productivity High need satisfaction	–	+	"lose-win"
"minus-minus" Low job productivity Low need satisfaction	–	–	"lose-lose"

Figure 3.1. The four possible types of relationships that can occur in the workplace. Management should strive to create the ++(win-win) relationship, as it leads to the greatest worker productivity and satisfaction. (The +– (win-lose) and –+(lose-win) relationships can occur for short periods of time, but they create imbalances between the needs of management and labor, usually resulting in the development of a – – condition. This lose-lose relationship occurs, sadly, all too often in the present-day workplace. It should be eliminated if business is to survive.

Why worry about satisfying employee needs anyway? One reason for this emphasis is my belief in human dignity: the assumption that management has a moral obligation to treat people as individuals, not objects. But for those who would label me a "bleeding heart" and rail at the "wastefulness" of this approach, let me emphatically say that such a practice is eminently pragmatic (economically sound).

Study after study, from automobile assembly lines to major department stores, reveals that managers who know how to satisfy workers—how to fulfill their needs—are those who get superior performance from their employees. And no wonder! It has long been known and accepted that to sell your product you must satisfy your customers' needs. Is it so surprising, then, that to sell production to your workers you must satisfy their needs?

The bottom line is clear: humanism and productivity are not incompatible. We can no longer afford to squander our human resources. We must learn to improve the morale and productivity of the workers so that we can effectively compete from a position of strength in the new world economy. Highly respected business expert John Gardner warns that ". . . we must discover how to design organizations and technological systems in such a way that individual talents are used to the maximum, and human satisfaction and dignity are preserved. We must learn to make technology serve man not only in the end product, but in the doing."[4]

Although my appeal for establishing + + relationships may sound revolutionary, it isn't. As a matter of fact, the + + concept has been around for quite a while, although judging from current management practices, it seems to have been largely ignored or forgotten. Frederick Taylor, the father of scientific management, had a basic appreciation of the + + relationship when he spoke of his "mental revolution," in which labor and management would work harmoniously to maximize profits rather than argue about how they should be divided.

The problem is, of course, how you as a manger can go about creating a + + work environment. It requires a lot of effort, application of the behavioral science principles presented in Section 2, and a belief that work can be something more than a four-letter word. It also involves developing a different conception of the *power relationships* between management and labor, a topic we will turn to in the next chapter. In the meantime you might want to read and ponder the passage in Box 3.1. It seems that young Tom Sawyer had a keen understanding of (and appreciation for) the + + relationship, which he set out to use in creating a win-win situation on the job.

Box 3.1
Brushing Up on the Plus-plus Relationship

Sometimes a job that seems devoid of any satisfaction can, with skillful management, be made to appear in a different light. Case in point: Tom Sawer and his famous fence-painting encounter. How he got out of doing the job (which he didn't want in the first place) and, most important, got someone else interested in doing it makes interesting reading in the context of the + + relationship.

We pick up the story where Ben, Tom's friend, spots him whitewashing the fence.

> "Hello, old chap, you got to work, hey?" Tom wheeled suddenly and said:
> "Why, it's you. Ben! I warn't noticing."
> "Say—I'm going in a-swimming, I am. Don't you wish you could? But of course you'd druther *work*—wouldn't you? course you would!"
> Tom contemplated the boy a bit, and said: "What do you call work?"
> "Why, ain't *that* work?"
> Tom resumed his whitewashing, and answered carelessly:
> "Well, maybe it is, and maybe it ain't. All I know is, it suits Tom Sawyer."

---

4. Ibid., p. 9.

"Oh, come now, you don't mean to let on that you *like* it?"

The brush continued to move.

"Like it? Well, I don't see why I oughtn't to like it. Does a boy get a chance to whitewash a fence every day?"

That put the thing in a new light. Ben stopped nibbling his apple. Tom swept his brush daintily back and forth—stepped back to note the effect—added a touch here and there— criticized the effect again—Ben watching every move and getting more and more interested, more and more absorbed. Presently he said:

"Say, Tom, let *me* whitewash a little."

Tom considered, was about to consent; but he altered his mind:

"No—no—I reckon it wouldn't hardly do, Ben. You see, Aunt Polly's awful par- ticular abot this fence—right here on the street, you know—but if it was the back fence I wouldn't mind and *she* wouldn't. Yes, she's awful particular about this fence; it's got to be done very careful; I reckon there ain't one boy in a thousand, maybe two thousand, that can do it the way it's got to be done."

"No—is that so? Oh come, now—lemme just try. Only just a little—I'd let *you*, if you was me, Tom."

"Ben, I'd like to, honest injun; but Aunt Polly. . . . If you was to tackle this fence and anything was to happen to it—"

"Oh, shucks, I'll be just as careful. Now lemme try. Say—I'll give you the core of my apple."

"Well, here—No, Ben, now don't. I'm afeard—"

"I'll give you *all* of it!"

Tom gave up the brush with reluctance in his face, but alacrity in his heart. And while . . . Ben . . . worked and sweated in the sun, the retired artist sat on a barrel in the shade close by, dangled his legs, and munched on his apple . . .*

*From Mark Twain, *The Adventures of Tom Sawyer*.

A New Conception of Managerial Power and Labor-Management Relations

4

I believe in power; but I believe that responsibility should go with power.

Theodore Roosevelt

In this chapter I want to talk with you about the power—the ultimate power—to influence human behavior. This brings to mind a demonstration popular in college classrooms. At the beginning of class the professor introduces a Dr. Hans Schmidt to the students, informing them that the guest is a "research chemist of international renown currently employed by the United States government to study the properties of gas diffusion." Dr. Schmidt, clad in a full-length white lab coat and sporting a well-tended goatee, then steps forward and, in a heavy German accent, tells the class he wishes to test the properties of a new chemical vapor he has developed. "Specifically," he says, "I wish to determine how quickly the vapor diffuses throughout the room and how readily people can detect it."

Pointing to a small glass beaker the doctor continues:

> Therefore I would ask your cooperation in a little experiment. I am going to pull this stopper and release the vapor. It is completely harmless but purposely treated to smell like gas—the kind you smell around a stove when the burner doesn't ignite. This particular sample is highly odorous so no one should have any trouble detecting its presence. What I want you to do is raise your hand as soon as you smell the vapor. Are there any questions?

At this point the chemist pulls the stopper and releases the vapor. Very soon, and in a very orderly manner, hands begin going up—first in the front rows and then on back—like a wave rolling through the lecture hall.

Obviously satisfied, the visiting scientist replaces the stopper, thanks the class for its cooperation, and leaves the room. Later on the professor informs his class that the "chemist" was in reality a faculty member from the German Department and the "vapor" nothing more than odorless distilled water.

Why, then, did nearly everyone smell gas? Power of suggestion, you might answer. Certainly the power of suggestion had something to do with it—but that wasn't the only or most important factor at work. Do you think, for example, that a student getting up before the class and making the same appeal could have received the same response as Dr. Schmidt? I've tried it: the answer is no. The power of suggestion worked so well because it was backed up by the *authority of the person making the suggestion. After all, didn't a famous chemist say the gas would be odorous and readily detected? A German* chemist at that (we all know how good German scientists are), wearing a white lab coat and referred to by the title of *Dr.* Schmidt.

The Authority Figure as a Power Source

Yes, Dr. Schmidt had all the trappings we associate with an *authority figure*—and a person perceived as an authority can be very persuasive indeed. As a matter of fact, authority figures have tremendous power in our society: they can mold opinions, command obedience, regulate the behavior of others. The most telling and awesome demonstration of this fact was provided by a social psychologist in a series of celebrated experiments at Yale University.

In the early 1960s Dr. Stanley Milgram had been wondering about the role of obedience in man's inhumanity to man, particularly the kinds of inhuman atrocities committed by the Nazis who were "acting under orders." Could the same obedience that made a child dutifully obey his parents and respond in socially acceptable fashion be turned around to make a person commit antisocial acts at the prodding of another authority figure? Dr. Milgram went into his laboratory to find out.

The Milgram experiment was a masterpiece of simplicity and deception. Two subjects were ushered into the laboratory to participate in a "learning experiment, ostensibly designed to study the effect of punishment on memory." One subject was to be the "teacher," the other the "learner." The subjects drew lots to determine their roles, but unbeknown to one of them, the drawing was rigged. One participant, the naive subject, was always given the role of the teacher; the other subject, a confederate of the experimenter, was given the role of the learner.

Once the drawing was completed, the learner was strapped into an "electric chair" and outfitted with electrodes capable of delivering powerful electric shocks to his body. The teacher, after observing this macabre scene, was ushered into an adjacent room containing an intercom and an imposing "shock generator." The generator, an impressive array of dials and switches, was outfitted with a control panel that gave the voltage readings for thirty separate levers (voltage levels went up in 15-volt steps, from 15 to 450 volts). Subjective descriptions of shock intensity were also included on the panel, ranging from Slight Shock at the lower intensities to Danger: Severe Shock at the 400-volt level. To convince the teacher of the authenticity of the shock generator and also to let him experience the painful properties of shock, he was administered a 45-volt stimulation.

The teacher's instructions were quite simple. He was told to teach the learner a list of word pairs over the intercom and punish him with an electric shock whenever he made a mistake, increasing the shock intensity one level (15 volts) for each new mistake. As the experiment progressed, the learner purposely made errors so that the teacher would have to shock him with increasingly severe shocks. As the shock level went up, the learner often made "increasingly insistent demands that the experiment be stopped because of the growing discomfort to him."

Although the teacher didn't realize it, *the learner never received any shocks.* Nor were his pleas real; they were in actuality a tape recording preprogrammed to deliver specific inputs when certain shock levels were reached. "They started with a grunt at 75 volts, proceeded through a 'Hey, that really hurts,' at 125 volts, got desperate with 'I can't stand the pain don't do that' at 180 volts, reached complaints of heart trouble at 195 (the learner had informed the teacher and the experimenter that he had heart trouble before the experiment began), an agonized scream at 285, a refusal to answer at 315, and only heartrending, ominous silence after that."[1]

If the teacher became concerned with the learner's agony, the experimenter ordered him to continue and to disregard the learner's protests. If the teacher balked and tried to quit, the experimenter commanded, "You have no choice, you must go on!" It should be emphasized that the

---

1. P. Meyer, "If Hitler Asked You to Electrocute a Stranger, Would You? Probably," *Esquire*, February 1970, p. 130.

teacher was free to quit the experiment and leave whenever he wanted to; the only way the experimenter could try and keep him at the task was by verbal commands that he must go on.[2]

The teacher's performance score was the highest level of shock intensity he was willing to administer to the learner. Thus his score could range from 0 (unwilling to administer any shock) to 450 (for a subject who gave the highest voltage on the shock generator).

When Dr. Milgram began his experiment, using townspeople from New Haven, Connecticut, he didn't expect many of the teachers to administer very high shocks to the learners. "I'll tell you quite frankly, before I began this experiment, before any shock generator was built, I thought that most people would break off at 'Strong Shock' (135–180 volts) or 'Very Strong Shock' (195–240 volts). You would get only a very, very small proportion of people going out to the end of the shock generator (450 volts), and they would constitute a pathological fringe."[3]

Dr. Milgram's colleagues and his students agreed with his assessment. In fact, when he asked a class of Yale University psychology students to estimate how many of a hypothetical group of a hundred subjects would give the most intense (450-volt) shock, the average answer was 1.2 percent. In other words, the Yale students felt that less than two subjects in a hundred would remain in the experiment to the end.

If only Dr. Milgram and his students had been correct! Unfortunately, their optimistic faith in human nature would find no support in the obedience study. Of the first forty subjects tested not *one* quit the experiment prior to administering 300 volts (at which point the learner is kicking the wall in agony); and twenty-six of the forty teachers (over 60 percent of the subjects tested) obeyed the experimenter to the end, punishing the hapless learner with the full 450 volts.

Many of these teachers displayed extreme tension and misgivings about their behavior, but when prodded on by the stern voice of the experimenter/authority over the intercom, they went on shocking the hell out of the protesting learner.

How much power do authority figures wield in this society? Listen to Dr. Milgram's summary of what he observed in his laboratory: "With numbing regularity, good people were seen to knuckle under to the demands of authority and perform actions that were callous and severe. . . . A substantial proportion of people do what they are told to do, irrespective of the content of the act and without limitations of conscience, so long as they perceive that the command comes from a legitimate authority."[4]

Managerial Authority and Power

There is no doubt that many people who hold positions of respect and authority can and *do* exert powerful control over the behavior of their fellow citizens. This brings us to the topic of managerial authority and power.

Managers, by the very nature of their position in society, have a degree of authority which gives them power in dealing with their subordinates. There are two reasons for this.

---

2. If the teacher expressed concern that he might be held liable for anything that happened to the learner, the experimenter could also attempt to keep him in the study by saying he (the experimenter) would take responsibility for anything that happened.

3. P. Meyer, op. cit., p. 128

4. Stanley Milgram, "Some Conditions of Obedience and Disobedience to Authority," *Human Relations*, vol. 18, 1965, pp. 74–75.

1. The title "manager" carries with it a built-in recognition of legitimate authority, particularly for those working within the business hierarchy.
2. Managers have a degree of "fate control" over their subordinates (for instance, hiring, firing, promotion, discipline) which lends credence to their position as authority figures.

As a manager you, like Dr. Schmidt and Dr. Milgram, will have the authority to control the behavior of your subordinates to a certain degree, depending in part on how effectively you utilize your power in the work environment.

But, is a manager's power absolute? That is, can managers control workers' behavior at will—totally, without challenge?

The answer is no. As a manager you are not the only power factor in a worker's life. There are other persons and institutions that the worker also respects, and those other sources of authority and power can also influence the worker's behavior (see Figure 4.1).

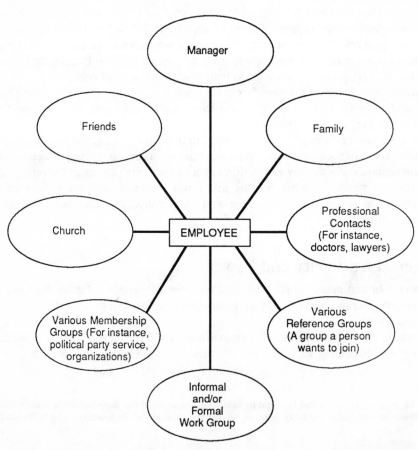

Figure 4.1. Some examples of power sources that can influence a worker's behavior.

At various times any or all of these other power sources can influence your employees' behavior; but, for all practical purposes, the only power sources that need concern us here are those of the manager and the work group (see Figure 4.2). It is between manager and work group that the potential for power conflict and cohesion are greatest; we will therefore examine this most critical relationship in greatest detail.

The Work Group as a Power Source

How many of you have taken a new job and experienced the tug-of-war feeling that occurs when your boss wants you to behave one way and your new coworkers want you to behave another? You're caught right in the middle—a very unpleasant and unfortunately not very uncommon experience.

I vividly remember just such an experience, even though it happened to me long ago. Having taken a summer job on a loading dock, I reported to work the first day and was assigned to load 50-pound sacks of grass seed into a large van. I took to the task with the enthusiasm of a new employee wanting to prove himself to management.

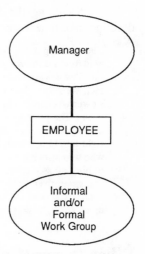

Figure 4.2. The major power focus in the workplace.

Only 2 hours into the workday a fellow employee approached me and suggested that I might be working a bit too fast. This message was delivered in a very effective manner: the 6-foot 6-inch, 250-pound old-timer hoisted all 165 pounds of me into the air and shook me like a rag doll while communicating his recommendation for a work slowdown. Needless to say, I complied with his wishes, and, after checking my body for wear and tear, I returned to the sack loading at a significantly reduced pace. Chalk one up for the work group as a power source!

As a manager you must remember that all groups—including work groups—attempt to regulate members' behavior by the application of rewards and punishments. That is, the individual group member is rewarded for conforming to the standards of the group and punished for deviating from them. sometimes the rewards and punishments are highly structured, formal, and clearly understood, as in the military. Other times they are more flexible, informal, and open to interpretation, as in the academic profession.

Work groups in industrial plants are notorious for their application of rewards and punishments to keep members in line. These sanctions are so powerful they often take precedence over the reward and punishment system imposed by management in the same plant.

Consider, for example, a classic series of studies at the Hawthorne Division of Western Electric Company in about 1930. One such investigation focused on a bank wiring room, where a group of fourteen workers (nine wiremen, three solderers, and two inspectors) assembled terminal banks for use in telephone exchanges. These workers were paid on the incentive system—the more they produced, the more they were paid.

The assumption behind the wage system was simple enough: every employee would work harder to amass a higher wage. The system failed. Why? Because the informal social organization of the workers in the bank wiring room had established a more powerful set of rewards and punishments (than money) to keep output at a fixed level and successfully challenge the power of management.

23

In discussing the Western Electric investigations, George C. Homans gives an excellent description of how work-group sanctions operate to control the behavior of individual laborers:

> The working group had also developed methods of enforcing respect for its attitudes. The experts who devised the wage incentive scheme assumed that the group would bring pressure to bear upon the slower workers to make them work faster and so increase the earnings of the group. In point of fact, something like the opposite occurred. The employees brought pressure to bear not upon the slower workers but upon the faster ones, the very ones who contributed most of the earnings of the group. The pressure was brought to bear in various ways. One of them was "binging." If one of the employees did something which was not considered quite proper, one of his fellow workers had the right to "bing" him. Binging consisted of hitting him a stiff blow on the upper arm. The person who was struck usually took the blow without protest and did not strike back. Obviously the virtue of binging as punishment did not lie in the physical hurt given to the worker but in the mental hurt that came from knowing that the group disapproved of what he had done. Other practices which naturally served the same end were sarcasm and the use of invectives. If a person turned out too much work, he was called names, such as "Speed King" or "The Slave."[5]

When Powers Collide

On the one hand, you as a manager possess power to influence the actions of your subordinates. On the other hand, work groups also have power which can be brought to bear on employee behavior. You can be sure that at certain times (often many times) during your career, the interests of the work group (or individual workers) and your interests as manager will be "out of sync," in opposition, in conflict. When this happens, we have a situation in which *powers collide*. Such power conflicts will truly test your mettle as a human resource director, for, in the final analysis, skillful handling of your power and the power of your subordinates is what effective managerial leadership is all about. How should you deal with such power problems? What are your options? You have several.

1 You Can Give in to the Opposing Power

What this means, basically, is that you acquiesce to the demands of the work group.[6] At times this is not a bad strategy. Capitulation to work-group power, if done appropriately, can make a manager look flexible, compassionate, and understanding of employees' needs. Also, in the long run of business operations, managers can afford to lose a few skirmishes with employees as long as they win the major battles. I know managers who purposely lose certain labor-management struggles so that they will be in a better position to gain their employees' allegiance on major issues.

The problem, however, with yielding to work-group demands *too* often is an undermining of managerial power. Managers who consistently adopt the "give in" strategy in labor-management power conflicts are seen as weak and ineffectual, and eventually lose any semblance of authority on the job.

5. G. Homans, "The Western Electric Researches," in Hoslett (ed.) *Human Factors in Management*, Harper, New York, 1951.

6. In this section I speak of power conflicts between you as manager and the work group; however, these options also hold true in a power conflict between you and an individual worker.

2 You Can Fight Power with Power

Here, the managers' strength is pitted against that of the work group and, as in a tug of war, the strongest power source pulls the opposing force "screaming and dragging their feet" across the finish line. Again, as in the case of the yielding strategy, fighting power with power is a workable policy *at times*. Used properly (and not too often) it can lead to increased worker respect for a manager and also compliance with specified orders.

Now for the difficulties. The problems with pitting power against power are potentially even more lethal than those encountered with the compliance approach. First of all, it can be a tremendous drain of energy for both labor and management, leaving little strength for job-relevant productivity. Secondly, the manager may lose the power struggle, and at that point the manager's authority will be seriously (if not irreparably) damaged. Finally, the manager may win the power battle and still lose the productivity war. Workers who are "beaten" into compliance often exhibit signs of bitterness and hostility long after the power struggle has ostensibly ended. This can lead to all kinds of critical management headaches—including loss of employee morale, reduced productivity, higher absenteeism and job turnover, and in extreme cases even physical confrontations with the manager or sabotage in the workplace.

3 You Can Reach a Compromise with the Opposing Power

Compromise means that nobody is a total winner, but, then, nobody is a total loser either. As a strategy for dealing with power confrontations, compromise can be effective in getting things accomplished and maintaining the peace, particularly if other power alternatives have been attempted and found unsuccessful.

Yet there is a major difficulty with the compromise approach: used too frequently, it often leads to a feeling on the part of management and labor alike that their needs are not being met. One business manager put it this way: "Compromise is a lot like having Chinese food—you eat it, but ten minutes later you feel hungry again."

4 You Can Harness the Opposing Power

When you harness the opposing power, you are basically using it to accomplish your own goals. This is not easily achieved, but if it can be done, it is the *best* way to deal consistently with conflicts of power.

In a business context the best method of harnessing the opposing power is to convince workers or work groups that it is in their best interest to carry out the actions that you, the manager, wish them to perform. Tom Sawyer did this with a flourish in the example presented in Box 3.1. You will be able to do it, too, once you put into practice the behavioral science techniques you will be learning in Section 2.

Harnessing employee power for your own ends might seem strange and new in business, but there is, in fact, nothing unusual or novel in this approach. There are many physical and human examples of this process—for instance, in the harnessing (with dams) of water power for electricity or the use of solar energy to heat homes and offices. Practitioners of the martial arts have long recognized that you can turn another person's power to your service. Thus, an individual skilled in the art of self-defense will readily utilize the attacking thrust of an adversary's arm to help throw the opponent off balance or to the ground.

Harnessing Power and the Plus-Plus Relationship

In Chapter 3 I spoke of the need to establish a + + relationship in the workplace—a condition whereby the needs of management and labor are both fulfilled; specifically, a condition in which productivity (management goal) and need satisfaction (employee goal) coexist. I suggested that until the + + goal was met, relations between labor and management would be strained and work would continue to be viewed as a four-letter word.

In the present discussion, you can now see how important establishment of the + + relationship becomes. Without the development of this win-win environment, suspicion and hostility between employee and employer will persist. As a matter of fact, the idea of harnessing worker power seems so farfetched in the business world exactly because of the antagonistic historical relationship that has evolved between manager and subordinate—making the idea of mutual cooperation seem unworkable, even unthinkable.

As long as this "adversarial" posture endures, the chance of harnessing worker power will remain remote. There will be too much distrust, too much hostility, too much of a win-lose attitude. It is only through the creation of the + + relationship that the old conceptions will give way to a more cooperative labor-management relationship, paving the way for you as future managers to harness worker power in the service of higher productivity.

A New Model for Labor-Management Relations

Steps must be taken, and taken now, to find the formula for establishing the + + relationship, for reducing conflict between labor and management—a productivity-draining interaction we can no longer afford in the light of current economic realities. One person who has taken such a step—and it is a giant one—is Muzafer Sherif, who, like Stanley Milgram, is a social psychologist. In the 1950s, Dr. Sherif conducted an innovative experiment with groups that, in my opinion, represents the most important psychological contribution ever made to the understanding of how to reduce hostility between labor and management and establish a healthy + + business environment. First let me present the experiment, and then I'll discuss its importance for contemporary management-labor relations.

The Sherif Experiment

Every year hundreds of thousands of city kids make their annual migration to that treasured American institution, the summer camp. There they swim, fish, shoot, canoe, learn arts and crafts, and go on overnights. At a camp in Oklahoma they unknowingly became experimental subjects in Dr. Sherif's study of intergroup relations.

A psychology experiment in a summer camp? It sounds strange. Yet, in actuality, Dr. Sherif chose this particular "laboratory" for sound scientific reasons: isolated from the outside world, the summer campsite provided a place where scientific control could be more readily achieved, a place where Sherif and his staff could manipulate the environment and observe the campers in a naturalistic setting, without fear that disturbances from the outside world would confound their results.

The campers that Sherif chose for his experiment were a counselor's dream: twenty-two healthy, well-adjusted 11-year-old boys, all from stable, middle-class families and in the upper half of their classes in scholastic standing. None of the boys had been problem children at home, in the neighborhood, or in school. They were basically peaceful preteenagers. Yet in a matter of weeks, they would be aggressively embroiled in a full-scale camp war under the watchful eye of the camp staff.

The camp war did not occur accidentally, it was an outgrowth of carefully planned experimental manipulations designed to help Dr. Sherif answer two basic questions: (1) How does intergroup conflict arise? (2) How can such conflict be reduced? In answering these inquiries, Dr. Sherif divided his camp study into three basic parts.

1 Stage of Group Formation Before you can study intergroup relations, you have to have groups. In the group-formation stage, two independent cohesive groups were created. This involved, first, an attempt by Dr. Sherif and his staff to divide the twenty-two campers into two equal units, making sure that the physical skills and sizes of the campers were roughly equivalent in each unit. Once this was done, the boys were transported, in separate buses, to opposite ends of the campsite and billeted in separate cabins. Then, for about a week the boys in each cabin participated in activities designed to foster the growth of well-developed groups. These activities included canoe trips over rough terrain and cookout overnights, the kinds of highly appealing tasks that require concerted, cooperative effort to carry out and build espirt de corps among the participants. Once each cabin unit had developed into a well-defined group, both groups were brought together for the first time, and the second stage of the experiment commenced.

2 Stage of Intergroup Conflict Just as you cannot study intergroup relations without groups, neither can you study the reduction of intergroup conflict without first producing that conflict. The question is, "How do you go about producing conflict between two groups of campers who are basically well-behaved and peaceful?" Dr. Sherif gives us an important hint with the following hypothesis:

> When members of two groups come into contact with one another in a series of activities that embody goals which each urgently desires, but which can be attained by one group only at the expense of the other, competitive activity toward the goal changes, over time, into hostility between the groups and their members.[7]

Now what "series of activities" can be conducted at a summer camp that "embody goals which each [group] urgently desires, but which can be attained by one group only at the expense of the other"? For those of you who have been to camp, one answer probably comes to mind immediately: a color war. For those unfamiliar with this term, a color war is a kind of junior Olympics, a time when the camp is divided into teams (each team designated by a color) that compete in a series of athletic events lasting from a day to a week or more. When all the events are completed, the team with the highest total score wins the color war. As any camper or counselor who has gone through such an experience will attest, a color war creates a fierce sense of competition and team pride that permeates the whole camp while the contest is in progress.

Making use of the color war potential for creating intergroup hostility, Dr. Sherif and the camp staff arranged for the boys of the two cabins to oppose each other in a tournament that included baseball, football, tent pitching, and tug-of-war contests. Observes Dr. Sherif:

> The tournament started with a great deal of zest and in the spirit of good sportsmanship to which these American boys had already been thoroughly indoctrinated. . . . As the tournament progressed from event to event, the good sportsmanship and good feeling began to evaporate. The sportsman-

7. Cited in M. Karlins and E. Hargis, "An Historical Psychological Framework Appropriate for a Contemporary Model of Labor-Management Relations," *Psychological Reports,* 1987, 60, p. 1045.

like cheer for the other group, customarily given after a game, "2-4-6-8, who do we appreciate," turned to a derisive chant: "2-4-6-8, who do we apprec*ihate*."[8]

In a very short time, what had begun as friendly relations between two groups of peaceful boys deteriorated into an intercabin donnybrook, replete with name-calling, fisticuffs, cabin raids, and property destruction. Dr. Sherif notes: "If an outside observer had entered the situation after the conflict began . . . he could only have concluded on the basis of their behavior that these boys (who were the 'cream of the crop' in their communities) were either disturbed, vicious, or wicked youngsters."[9] That's how bad things got.

There was no question about it: Intergroup conflict had been solidly achieved at Dr. Sherif's summer camp. The problem now was to end it. The whole purpose of the experiment was to find a way of reducing intergroup conflict; and judging from the behavior of Dr. Sherif's campers, there would never be a better time to find the solution.

3 Reduction of Intergroup Conflict Through experimental manipulation, Dr. Sherif had first created conditions conducive to the formation of groups and then to the onset of hostilities between them. Now, in the final stage of the experiment, Dr. Sherif set out to answer this question: "How can two groups in conflict, each with hostile attitudes and negative images of the other and each desiring to keep the members of the detested outgroup at a safe distance, be brought into cooperative interaction and friendly intercourse?"

Several approaches were tried. One approach was an *appeal to the moral values* shared by members of both groups. This appeal was contained in sermons given by the camp minister at religious services. In these sermons, he talked of brotherly love, the value of cooperation, and the need for forgiving one's enemies. "The boys arranged the services and were enthusiastic about the sermons," Dr. Sherif writes. Nevertheless, "upon solemnly departing from the ceremony, they returned within minutes to their concerns to defeat, avoid, or retaliate against the detested outgroup."[10]

A second approach involved *bringing the groups together at events that were very enjoyable.* Thus, the groups were brought together to eat, see movies, shoot off fireworks on the Fourth of July, and so forth. Unfortunately, this approach also failed. "Far from reducing conflict, these situations served as occasions for the rival groups to berate and attack each other. . . . The mealtime encounters were dubbed 'garbage wars' by the participants,"[11] who used their food for ammunition rather than nourishment.

The one approach that Dr. Sherif believed would work—*and did*—involved the use of *superordinate goals* in the reduction of intergroup conflict. "Superordinate goals are those goals that have a compelling appeal for members of each group, but that neither group can achieve without participation of the other."[12]

To demonstrate that accomplishing superordinate goals leads to reduced intergroup hostility, Dr. Sherif and his staff rigged the camp program so that highly desirable activities and outcomes could be realized only through the joint cooperation of the two groups. For example, one day on an outing, the two groups of boys were faced with a terrible problem: Hot, tired, and hungry, they reached their campsite only to discover that the truck which was to go for food and water was

8. Ibid.
9. Ibid., p. 1046.
10. Ibid.
11. Ibid.
12. Ibid.

stalled and needed to be pulled onto the road. One group of campers got a rope, tied it around the truck's fender, and began to tug. The vehicle didn't move, and it became obvious that one group working alone couldn't accomplish the task. When both groups pulled on the rope together, however, they were able to get the truck started and on its way.

Joint efforts in situations such as the stalled truck episode did not immediately dispel hostility between the two groups. "But gradually," Dr. sherif notes, "the series of activities requiring interdependent action reduced conflict and hostility between the groups. . . . In the end, the groups were actively seeking opportunities to intermingle, to entertain and 'treat' each other."[13]

All's well that ends well. On the last day of the camp session, the boys were given the choice of returning home together on one bus or on two separate buses, one for each group. They voted to return together.

Superordinate Goals and Labor-Management Relations

From peace to war and back to peace again. At least in his summer camp, Dr. Sherif seemed to create conflict or cooperation at his bidding. Now nobody is suggesting that what Dr. Sherif did with a group of boys in Oklahoma he could do as easily with labor and management. But what Dr. Sherif learned about the induction and reduction of intergroup hostility might very well be applicable to improving labor-management relations.

In contemporary business, we are confronting productivity problems that can be solved only through the *cooperation* of labor and management. Just as Dr. sherif's campers could not move the truck without intergroup cooperation, neither can we move the economy forward without the cooperation of employer and employee working together.

This currently leaves us in an extremely ironical state of affairs. Labor and management are, in fact, partners in progress—they are irrevocably yoked together in a common effort to survive and prosper. One can not succeed without the other. Yet, through the years these two groups have behaved as if they were natural foes, enemies to be defeated.

Please don't get me wrong. I am not saying that it is unhealthy or unnatural to allow an "adversarial" position between labor and management (the Western nations have squabbles even though they are allies). Disagreements and differences of opinion can be healthy to all parties, if carried out in the proper spirit and context. What I am saying is that as future managers your perception of labor-management relations (one you should attempt to transmit to labor and one which labor should embrace as well) should be more in keeping with the true reality of the situation. Labor and management are like Siamese twins, joined together in a struggle for survival. You can't cut off one half and expect the other half to survive and prosper.

Management and labor should think in terms of cooperation rather than conflict, harmony rather than tension. Business presents employer and employee with a "natural" superordinate goal. It would be a shame if labor and management didn't grasp at the opportunity to cooperate in the achievement of that goal.

Remember the all-important Sherif hypothesis:

When members of two groups come into contact with one another in a series of activities that embody goals which each urgently desires, but which can be attained by one group only at the expense of the other, competitive activity toward the goal changes, over time, into hostility between the groups and their members.

13. Ibid.

It would be the height of unnecessary tragedy if labor and management waste their energy fighting each other on the mistaken assumption that only one group can win at the expense of the other, when in fact the only way either group can win is through the mutual cooperation of both.[14]

As long as management and labor insist on viewing their interaction in terms of a win-lose situation, only a lose-lose result can occur, particularly in today's world, where business faces harsher international competition than ever before. When, on the other hand, both groups come to see their roles as cooperative, interdependent and win-win in nature, then the potential for a productive ++ relationship will be enhanced, along with the opportunity for management to effectively harness worker power in the service of higher productivity.

14. Ibid., p. 1047.

SECTION TWO

**Theory Goes to Work:
How to Be an Effective
Human Resource Manager
in the Real World**

The Need to Know

5

The need to know is your employee's need.

First-line supervisor

Having just finished the theoretical section of this book, you now have a philosophical and conceptual basis for effective human resource management. But, I hear you asking, how can I apply that theory in practice and make myself a more effective manager on the job? In other words, how do I translate theoretical ideas into action programs in the workplace?

The answer is, by utilizing behavioral science techniques to satisfy worker needs and enhance worker output. I will be discussing these techniques in the next few chapters, showing you how to use them to harness worker power and create the + + relationship so vital to making the workplace a productive worthplace. First, however, you must know the following.

How to Understand and Identify Individual Worker Needs

Before you can satisfy worker needs, you must know what they are. If you think you already do, then spend a moment to take the test in Box 5.1.

Once you have finished taking the test (and not before!) I think you'll find it instructive to look at two other sets of responses: one from an actual group of employees, the other from a group of supervisors. *These responses can be found on the last page of this chapter.* Transfer your own estimates (from the test above) to the spaces provided at the end of the chapter and then make a few comparisons.

The employee rankings represent the actual expression of what a group of workers felt were important wants to be satisfied on the job. How did you do in comparison with their rankings? Did you accurately assess what they wanted most from their work? If you didn't, don't feel bad—you weren't alone. When you glance at the supervisors' ranking it's obvious that they, too, were way off when it came to guessing what workers want most on the job.

Commenting on these data, Professor Kenneth Kovach notes:

> The ranking of items is not necessarily the important thing to observe, since conditions have changed since . . . the survey was taken. The significant point is the wide variance between what workers consider to be important in their jobs and what their supervisors think workers believe to be important. Research indicates that a wide gap still exists between what workers want from their jobs and what management thinks they want.[1]

Unfortunately, it has been this management misreading of worker needs that has led to so many problems in labor-management relations now and in the past.

1. Kenneth Kovach, "Improving Employee Motivation in Today's Business Environment," *MSU Business Topics,* Autumn 1976, p. 7.

Test Directions

Below, you will find a list of 10 things people want from their work. Your task is to rank the items in order from 1 (most important) to 10 (least important) on the basis of how you think the average worker (not manager) would rate the items. In other words, try to predict how a worker would respond to the 10 items on the basis of their job-related needs.

Here are the 10 items. Remember, 1 is most important, 10 is least important.

Your Estimate of Worker's Ranking	What People Want From Their Work
_____	Full appreciation of work done
_____	Feeling of being in on things
_____	Sympathetic help on personal problems
_____	Job security
_____	Good wages
_____	Interesting work
_____	Promotion and growth in the organization
_____	Personal loyalty to employees
_____	Good working conditions
_____	Tactful disciplining

As I indicated earlier, to increase worker productivity you must satisfy worker needs, and to satisfy worker needs you must know what they are. Different workers have different needs at different times. If you can ascertain each employee's needs with accuracy, you'll be in a better position to satisfy the employee and encourage higher productivity on the job.

Assessing the needs of individual workers is not as difficult as it sounds. In the first place, many workers have the same needs. Then, there aren't that many different needs to worry about. Moreover, by conscientiously observing your employees you can usually ascertain their needs. Finally, behavioral scientists have provided us with some good "models" of human needs, models that will help you understand and assess workers' needs more accurately. Here I would like to present one such model: the so-called need hierarchy of Abraham Maslow.[2] Although the model is a gross oversimplification of complex human behavior and doesn't hold true for every employee you'll confront, it still provides us with some useful guidelines for identifying worker needs and understanding how they operate.

2. Abraham Maslow, *Motivation and Personality*, Harper, New York, 1954

The Maslow Model of Human Needs

Think for a moment: If I were to ask you to explain your behavior—to tell me why you pursued a certain goal or acted in a certain way—how would you answer? Abraham Maslow spent a career considering this kind of question, and here is how he would reply:

1. People have needs and they will act in ways to satisfy their needs. As long as our needs remain unfulfilled they act as *motivators*, stimulating us to behave in ways that will lead to the satisfaction of those needs. Once a need is satisfied, however, it no longer motivates a person and other unfulfilled needs take its place.
2. Some needs are more pressing (more important) than others. For instance, the need to breathe is more crucial than the need to gain public recognition for a job well done.
3. The basic, most survival-relevant needs must first be satisfied before other, more psychologically oriented needs become motivators of behavior. In other words, a person will seek to satisfy the rumblings of an empty stomach before turning to the challenges of an inquisitive mind.

It was Maslow's realization that human needs vary in importance and behavioral priorities which led him to postulate his "need hierarchy" concept (see Figure 5.1).

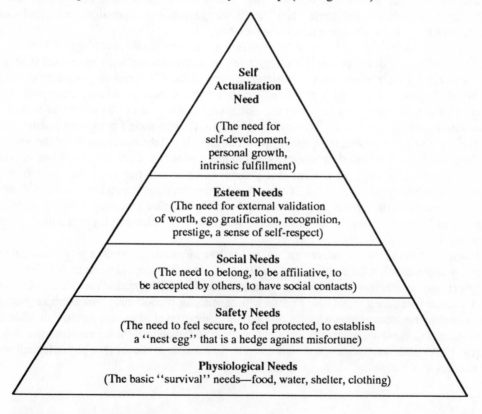

Figure 5.1. Maslow's hierarchy of human needs.

It will help you understand the need hierarchy if you view it as a kind of stepladder people climb on their way to total fulfillment as human beings.

The first rung on the ladder represents the *physiological needs*. These are very urgent needs that must be satisfied before any higher-rung needs can come into play. There are very few physiological needs, but they must be satisfied if the individual is to survive. Examples of these needs are air, water, food, and—in certain climates—clothing and shelter. In contemporary North America most people have been successful in satisfying their survival needs; but for the millions of people throughout the world who haven't, life is little more than a grim day-by-day struggle for survival.

The second rung on the ladder represents the *safety needs*. Once people have won the day-to-day struggle to stay alive, they start looking for longer-term solutions to the survival problem. People with safety needs are motivated to seek *security*: to protect themselves against misfortune and put distance between themselves and the daily scramble for survival.

The third rung on the ladder represents the *social needs*. Here the individual is concerned with *affiliation*: being around other people and being accepted by them. People with social needs want to belong—they desire social relationships and the chance to interact with others.

The fourth rung on the ladder represents *esteem needs*. People with esteem needs seek external validation of their worth; that is, they want others to recognize their competence and accomplishments. Individuals with these "ego" needs are concerned with prestige, status, and a sense of self-respect that comes with recognized achievement.

The fifth rung on the ladder is *self-actualization* and represents, according to Maslow, the highest level of human development. People with self-actualization needs are motivated to seek internal validation of their worth; that is, their values are defined in terms of personal beliefs and philosophies. People who attempt to self-actualize are striving to become all they are capable of becoming—in short, to reach their full potential as human beings. It is in this stage that individuals grapple with the age-old questions: Who am I? Where am I? Where am I going? Self-actualization is the pursuit of self-fulfillment, the quest for personal growth and the development of the total self.

From what I have just said, it becomes evident that a person's position on the Maslow hierarchy will determine, in large part, what that person wants out of life in general and from the workplace in particular (see Figure 5.2). Consider, for example, a person on the "first rung" of the Maslow hierarchy. Certainly this individual will be more satisfied receiving a living wage than recognition as "employee of the month." And, as we know, a satisfied employee is a more productive employee.

It is important to note that movement up the Maslow hierarchy of needs is progressive; that is, "lower" needs must first be satisfied before "higher" needs make themselves felt. Further, if people operating at a higher need level are suddenly confronted by conditions which push them back to a lower level, then those lower needs will once again predominate. An example: Suppose you're a wealthy business person who functions at the esteem level of human needs. One afternoon your pleasure boat is blown out to sea and suddenly you're forced to fight for survival on a day-to-day basis. Under such conditions you would revert to functioning at the level of physiological needs until the crisis was resolved.

What a Person Wants Out of Life	Maslow's Hierarchy of Needs	What a Person Wants Out of a Job
Freedom Personal growth (self-development) Achieve full human potential	Self-actualization needs	Creative and challenging work Responsibility for decision making Flexibility and freedom
Status Prestige Recognition for achievement	Esteem needs	Promotion Praise (recognition) by supervisor Merit pay increase
Social relationships Acceptance by others Affiliation	Social needs	Compatible work group Social activities at work Friendship at work
Security Safety "Nest egg"	Safety needs	Safe and healthy working conditions Job security Reasonable wages and fringe benefits
Food Water Clothing and shelter	Physiological needs	Meals Shelter from the elements Subsistence wages

Figure 5.2. What people want out of life and work at various levels of Maslow's need hierarchy.

Some Limitations of the Maslow Model

As I pointed out earlier, Maslow's need hierarchy isn't a precise scientific instrument for predicting human behavior; rather, it is a descriptive model that gives us general guidelines for classifying and understanding human needs.

When considering Maslow, you should be aware that not all people behave according to his model. For instance, some people are motivated by more than one need at a time—like the person who strives for social relationships (social need) and prestige (esteem need) at the same time. There are also people who don't fit into the five-step progression of needs in the need hierarchy. Some people skip over certain need levels entirely (as when a person moves from safety needs directly to esteem needs); others voluntarily move *down* the need hierarchy (for instance, well-paid executives who quit their jobs in favor of subsistence farming on an agricultural commune). Finally, there is the factor of *rising expectations*.

> As people partially satisfy each need, they tend to require more of it for full satisfaction. This . . . phenomenon of rising expectations . . . partially explains why workers today are unhappy with their earnings even though earnings have never been higher. A starving factory worker of the 1800s was overjoyed to earn enough to buy an extra potato. A factory worker today becomes angry if he cannot afford steak.[3]

3. Michael Mescon and David Rachman, *Business Today*, Random House, New York (new edition, in press).

So much for the limitations of the Maslow model. Even with such shortcomings, it can still be an extremely valuable ally in your efforts to manage more effectively. Do, however, keep those limitations in mind.

Using Maslow to Manage

A basic premise of this book can be expressed in the statement: *if you want worker productivity you must satisfy worker needs*. I began this chapter by suggesting that many contemporary managers can't satisfy worker needs because they don't know what they are. I then presented the Maslow model to help you understand the types of human needs and how they function, an understanding that should put you in a better position to identify your workers' needs more accurately. Let me explain why this is so.

Based on what Maslow has said, you now know the types of needs workers have and the corresponding factors that can be used to satisfy their needs step by step, starting with the basic physiological (survival) needs and moving up to the psychological needs of esteem and self-actualization.

Given this information, plus your knowledge of current economic conditions, you might well decide that most contemporary American workers will be motivated by higher (as opposed to lower) level needs. And you would be right. Of course, this wasn't always the case. In earlier times, when labor rights were nonexistent and wages desperately low, workers were not worried about gaining prestige or the opportunity for self-esteem—their concern was for survival and security, pure and simple.[4] With the rise of labor unions and social legislation, however, plus four decades of unpredecented prosperity, working conditions changed. Labor won better wages and job security. Many workers found their physiological and safety needs were satisfied—*and a satisfied need ceases to motivate an individual*. These workers began looking to different kinds of satisfaction, the needs for social interaction, esteem, and self-fulfillment. This quest continues into the 1990s. Of course, should economic conditions take a dramatic downturn to a point where survival or job security once again becomes a meaningful concern, then (as Maslow predicted) we can expect many workers to again be motivated by physiological and safety needs.

How Can I Identify My Own Workers' Needs?

In general, when it comes to today's workers you can be fairly certain (all things being equal) that most of your full-time employees will be striving to fulfill higher-level needs on the Maslow hierarchy.

Of course, there will always be exceptions to any general rule; and for that reason your ability to assess accurately any *specific* worker's needs will be improved if you get to know your employees individually and any personal circumstances that might affect their needs (see Chapter 6). For example, those who might normally be concerned with self-esteem will focus instead on security needs if they suddenly finds their financial nest egg destroyed by an unexpected (and costly) medical problem.

---

4. For a depiction of workers struggling to stay alive in early industrial America read Upton Sinclair's novel *The Jungle*.

Sometimes the only way to be sure about the particular needs of individual workers is to offer them several different on-the-job *rewards*, each designed to satisfy a different need on the Maslow hierarchy, and then watch to see which is the most effective. To do this successfully you'll want to learn more about which rewards go with which needs and how you can administer those rewards effectively in the workplace. This involves the use of behavior modification—a technique you can learn to use once you read Chapters 6, 7, and 8.

Employee and Supervisory Responses To Box 5.1 Test

What People Want from Their Work	Employee Ranking	Supervisor Ranking	Your Ranking
Full appreciation of work done	1	8	_____
Feeling of being in on things	2	10	_____
Sympathetic help on personal problems	3	9	_____
Job security	4	2	_____
Good wages	5	1	_____
interesting work	6	5	_____
Promotion and growth in the organization	7	3	_____
Personal loyalty to employees	8	6	_____
Good working conditions	9	4	_____
Tactful disciplining	10	7	_____

Give the Nod to Behavior Mod   6

"Behavior modification isn't magic, but it sure works like it on the job."

Manager of a fast-food restaurant

You can't satisfy worker needs if you don't know what they are. In Chapter 5 we found out what they are, and now we're ready to satisfy those needs through the use of *behavior modification,* a powerful and exciting behavioral science technique that is being utilized by a rapidly-expanding number of companies to fulfill worker needs and enhance worker productivity at the same time.

What Is Behavior Modification?

Behavior modification is a *scientific* procedure for systematically changing behavior through the use of rewards or punishments or both. Defined in such a manner, free of academic jargon, the method seems, to some people, to offer nothing new. In one sense, those people are correct: The man who purchases flowers for his wife or spanks his child is practicing a rudimentary form of behavior modification (rudimentary in comparison with the more sophisticated, systematic, and effective behavior modification used by scientists). Nevertheless, these people are incorrect in assuming that behavior modification is "old hat." What makes the approach novel (and effective) is the use of psychological learning principles in the reinforcement of behavior.

Although the major thrust of behavior modification only began in the 1960s, the impetus for the movement came from investigations in the earlier decades of this century. One classic and influential study was performed in 1920 by john Watson, father of psychological behaviorism and advocate of human behavior control. Watson was convinced that such control was feasible and, not one to hide his convictions, once boasted:

> Give me a dozen healthy infants, well formed, and my own specified world to bring them up in and I'll guarantee to take any one at random and train him to become any type of specialist I might select—doctor, lawyer, artist, merchant-chief, and, yes, even beggar-man and thief, regardless of his talents, penchants, tendencies, abilities, vocations, and race of his ancestors.[1]

Unlike many of his contemporaries who speculated on such matters but went no further, Watson set out to substantiate his claims in the laboratory. His proof was gathered at the expense of Albert, a normal, healthy infant. Albert was basically stolid and unemotional. He cried infrequently, didn't scare easily, and, except when confronted with loud sounds, showed no signs of fear. At 9 months of age, he was suddenly presented with objects he had never seen before including a white rat, a rabbit, a dog, a monkey, cotton, and wool; and he approached these objects without apprehension.

---

1. John Watson, *Behaviorism,* People's Institute, New York, 1924, p. 82.

41

At this juncture, Watson set out to prove his point: that he could control Albert's behavior at will and, specifically, make him afraid of the white rat he now approached fearlessly. The animal was admitted into Albert's playroom, as it had been before, but now each time the child reached for the animal, a loud gong was struck nearby. After a very few of these encounters, Albert began to cry and scurry away whenever he saw the rat, even when the gong did *not* sound. Furthermore, the child showed fear of the objects that looked like a rat, for example, the white rabbit he had earlier approached without fear. By a few pairings of a negative reinforcer (loud sound) with an initially attractive plaything, Watson was effectively able to condition little Albert's behavior and make him afraid of a whole class of objects similar to and including a white rat.[2]

My First Experience with Behavior Modification

I've always had an "I'm from Missouri . . . show me" attitude about things, so when I first heard about behavior modification as an undergraduate, my first reaction was skepticism. My second reaction was to test it and see what would happen. I was a psychology major and I remember thinking: If this really works, it should work for me. I checked with some of my classmates. They felt the same way. So, in the true spirit of science, we set out to see whether we could control human actions using behavior modification. Our little experiment was conducted on a particularly unpopular teacher, a chap we dubbed Mr. Monotone.

Mr. Monotone was the kind of instructor whose lectures should have been recorded and sold to hardcore insomniacs. I am sure the cure rate would have been astounding. Three times a week, an hour a day, he gave his dreadful little lectures, delivered in a dronelike monotone from a mouth that hardly seemed to move. To make matters worse, Mr. Monotone stood rigidly behind the podium and stared straight ahead when he spoke. In fact, the only real evidence that he was alive (besides the steady stream of words tumbling colorlessly from his lips) was his tendency to scratch his head with his left hand. This little gesture occurred five or six times an hour, usually at 8-to 10-minute intervals.

We decided to see if we could increase the frequency of Mr. Monotone's head-scratching gesture through behavior modification. First we enlisted the aid of a few students in his class (in addition to ourselves) to participate in the "investigation." Once everyone knew what to do, we situated ourselves in a row near the front of the class, and here's what we did: Every time Mr. Monotone lectured in his normal, motionless manner we showed no real interest in the lecture. But whenever he made his head-scratching gesture we immediately went into action, nodding our heads in approval, smiling, furiously scribbling notes—everything we could to reward Mr. Monotone with something we figured he needed; social approval.

Sure enough, in a matter of hours, Mr. Monotone was scratching his head like a dog with fleas. Not only did he scratch more frequently, but his hand stayed in his hair longer each time he did.

The results of our little study spoke well for the power of behavior modification to control certain kinds of behavior. It took only a few lectures before Mr. Monotone had increased his head scratching in response to our reward of social approval. Furthermore, when we ended the experiment (stopped giving approval for the head-scratching behavior), it gradually returned to its normal prereinforcement levels.

2. John Watson and R. Rayner, "Conditioned Emotional Reactions," *Journal of Experimental Psychology,* vol. 3, 1920, pp. 1–14.

Little Albert and Mr. Monotone Compared

John Watson's experiment with little Albert and our investigation with Mr. Monotone share one important characteristic: the use of *reinforcement* to change behavior. Behavior modification works by increasing or decreasing the likelihood of a specified behavioral response through systematic reward and punishment. Little Albert received negative reinforcement (loud sound), and it is assumed that such punishment will eventually lead to cessation of the negatively reinforced behavior. In the case of Mr. Monotone, the reinforcement was positive (social approval), and it is expected that rewarded behavior will be maintained (and often increase in frequency). The process by which reinforcement becomes associated with certain behaviors is called *conditioning*. The psychologist uses his knowledge of conditioning principles to make his efforts more effective.

One can get a feeling for the power of conditioning procedures, for how such methods can systematically change a wide variety of human actions, by reading B. F. Skinner's novel *Walden Two*. Although it is labeled a work of fiction, it is grounded in scientific facts, using the established learning principles underlying behavior modification to regulate human behavior and create a utopian community. In reality, the book is a reflection of Skinner's scientific thinking from start to finish, an application of his operant conditioning methods to the design of a society created and governed by psychologists.

In *Walden Two*, everyone is well-behaved, happy, and productive. Citizens are controlled, but they are not aware of being controlled. Control is achieved by procedures similar to those employed by Watson with little Albert and the undergraduates with Mr. Monotone. Explains the novel's psychologist-hero: "When he behaves as we want him to behave, we simply create a situation he likes, or remove one he doesn't like. As a result, the probability that he will behave that way again goes up, which is what we want. Technically it's called 'positive reinforcement.' "[3] *Walden Two* is deeply grounded in the principles of behavior modification.

In the years since the early work of Watson and Skinner, scientists have made behavior modification a far more powerful system for controlling behavior. At the same time, they have used it to change increasingly complex and diverse types of human activity. Some behavior modification takes place in clinical settings, where it is used to eliminate or modify dysfunctional personal behavior. The ability of behavior modification to change entrenched, highly resistant forms of human activity reminds us of its potency as a behavior control device.

Using Behavior Modification In the Workplace

It was only a matter of time before the behavior-changing power of behavior modification attracted the attention of the business community. Would the technique be effective in the workplace? Ask Emery Air Freight Corporation. As far back as the early, 1970s the company embarked on a pioneering behavior modification program which saved it over $2 million in 3 years.[4]

Part of the program centered on the customer service department, where employees were charged with the responsibility of answering all customer inquiries within a 90-minute time frame. (If you had a question about shipping rates, the goal of the customer service representative was to get back to you with an answer within 90 minutes.) When customer service representatives were

3. B. Skinner, *Walden Two*, Macmillan, New York, 1948.

4. Herbert Huebner and Alton Johnson, "Behavior Modification: An Aid in Solving Personnel Problems," *The Personnel Administrator*, October 1974, p. 34.

asked how often they met the 90-minute goal, their response was optimistic: 90 percent of the time. Research, however, revealed that the goal was being achieved only 30 percent of the time.

To try and improve employee performance, each customer service representative was asked to record the actual time it took to answer each incoming inquiry on a log sheet. The log sheets were then checked daily by management, and feedback was given to employees concerning how well they were doing. Anytime an employee showed improved performance (more calls answered within the 90-minute limit) they were *rewarded* with praise from their supervisor. Even those who didn't improve their performance received a reward of sorts: they were praised for their honesty and accuracy in filling out their log sheets and were then reminded of the 90-minute goal.

The results of the behavior modification program were dramatic. After a few days of feedback and praise, customer service representatives were meeting the 90-minute time limit 90 percent of the time — and some employees were even setting higher goals for themselves.

The same basic behavior modification design was utilized by Emery Air Freight Corporation in its shipping department. Using the log-sheet approach, shipping department employees monitored their performance and received feedback and praise from their supervisors. The result? Container-packing efficiency jumped from 45 percent to 90 percent, saving the company over half a million dollars per year in shipping costs.

How has the business community reacted to Emery Air Freight's pioneering experience with behavior modification? Being basically conservative, business leaders haven't suddenly embraced the technique as the ultimate cure-all. Yet the developments of the past decade make one thing clear: behavior modification will become an increasingly important management tool for shaping profits and worker satisfaction in the coming years. This should come as no surprise, particularly when you consider the increasing number of psychologists and psychologically trained managers entering the business world. They're familiar with the power of behavior modification, and they'll be in a position to use it on the job. No doubt they will, and I hope you do, too.

Institutional Versus Personal Behavior Modification Programs

In reality, there are two kinds of behavior modification programs that can be used in the workplace. One kind I call the *institutional* behavior modification program. Normally, such a program is a highly formalized, large-scale affair, requiring coordinating and directing skills that come from years of specialized education and training. If as a manager you should be asked to participate in such a program, feel free to do so. But I don't recommend that you *start* one. The responsibility for creating and directing institutional behavior modification programs is best left to professional consultants or in-house organizational development (OD) directors. They have the proper training for the job, you don't.

Do not despair, however. There is still the second kind of program, called the *personal* behavior modification program, that you *can* start; in fact, it is labeled personal because you can use it with your employees even if no other manager in the entire organization follows suit. And, best of all, you don't need the specialized skills of the trained psychologist or professional consultant to make a personal behavior modification program function effectively in the workplace.[5] What you

5. This is primarily because personal behavior modification programs (unlike institutional programs) do not present the complex design and coordination problems that require the attention of more highly trained personnel. Let's face it, there are many people who can serve up an excellent feast for ten to twenty guests at home, but that doesn't qualify them to walk into the local restaurant and prepare a banquet for six hundred.

do need is a willingness to commit some time and effort to the undertaking, a caring attitude toward your employees, an unwavering commitment to use behavior modification in an ethical manner and a set of guidelines for applying personal behavior modification on the job. Let us turn to those guidelines now.

How You Can Utilize Behavior Modification With Your Employees

From our discussion of Maslow's need hierarchy and the experiments in behavior modification, you now possess two vital pieces of information:

1. Individual workers have individual needs, and they will behave in ways that lead to the satisfaction of those needs.
2. Behavior that is rewarded will be maintained or will even increase in frequency.

Putting this information together, your goal as a manager is to reinforce appropriate work behavior with rewards that satisfy the particular needs of individual employees. This should enhance worker productivity and satisfy worker needs, thus establishing the ++ relationship essential to making the workplace a worthplace.

To accomplish this goal will require you to successfully complete a three-step process:

Step 1 You will have to identify the specific needs of your individual workers

Step 2 You will have to satisfy each worker's specific need(s) with the appropriate reward(s).

Step 3 You will have to administer worker rewards effectively.

Step 1, which has already been discussed in Chapter 5, will be examined again in the next few pages.

Step 2 will be discussed in Chapter 7, where you will find the various reinforcements you can use in motivating your workers. You can use any or all of these rewards, depending on your circumstances and the particular needs of your various employees.

Step 3 will be discussed in Chapter 8, where you will learn the basic rules for administering rewards in a manner that maximizes worker productivity and satisfaction.

A Final Note on Identifying Worker Needs

In Chapter 5 I gave you Maslow's behavioral science model to help you understand and identify your workers' needs more accurately. I also pointed out that many workers have the same needs, which tend to cluster on the higher rungs of the Maslow hierarchy. Thus, if you simply assume that *all* your employees have social, esteem and self-actualization needs, you'll probably be right in most instances.

If, however, you want to obtain greater accuracy in identifying your individual workers' needs, then it will be necessary to conscientiously observe them on the job. It doesn't take long to determine a worker's needs once you watch that person in action—in fact, once you have a little observational experience under your belt, you'll be amazed at just how quickly and accurately you can "read" an individual's needs.

Do you want to obtain the *greatest* accuracy in identifying your workers' needs? If so, observe your employees as you give them various rewards. That way you can pinpoint the reinforcements that work best for each employee. Such information is particularly valuable because, in most instances, you'll have to pick from a number of different rewards to use at any given need level of the Maslow hierarchy.

Finally, continue to observe your subordinates even *after* you have ascertained their needs and the rewards they value most. This is crucial, because workers' needs can change over time and so can their attitudes toward particular rewards. For example, some workers get bored with certain rewards if they're used too often, causing them to lose their effectiveness. If you continue to observe your subordinates, you will be alerted to these changes and be able to take corrective action. Otherwise you might miss such changes entirely and wonder why you ended up with a disgruntled, unproductive employee.

It is interesting to note that identifying worker needs with accuracy and practicing effective behavior modification both require the manager to pay *attention to the worker:* to observe, to be aware, to see (not look through) the people whom they supervise. I am not exaggerating when I say that paying attention to your employees is a basic prerequisite to becoming an effective human resource manager. Not only does it help you understand your workers, but it motivates them as well—as you shall soon see.

Fourteen Rewards You Can Use in the Workplace

7

"I feel more like working now that my manager seems to recognize my existence."

Shoe store salesperson

I'd like you to play scientist for a moment and consider what you'd do in the following circumstances.

Here is the situation. A major corporation has called you in to determine if variations in working conditions can influence employee productivity on the job. To find out, you begin by studying illumination in the workplace. Your hypothesis is simply enough: an increase in illumination will lead to an increase in productivity. Your experiment is simple, too. You designate one set of employees the test group and subject it to deliberate changes in illumination while it works; a second set of workers, called the control group, works under the original lighting throughout the experiment. The only problem is that the results are anything but simple; in fact, they are downright perplexing. Here is what you find:

1. Test group productivity rises when illumination is improved (increased)—as predicted by your hypothesis.
2. Test group productivity also rises when illumination is worsened (decreased). (No hypothesis ever predicted that!)
3. Output also increases in the control group—even though illumination remains constant. (Something definitely strange is going on here.)

All right, what do you do? If you answer, "Drop the experiment," you will be doing exactly what *was* done back in 1927 when a group of scientists from the Massachusetts Institute of Technology puzzled over the same results and finally abandoned the project. If, on the other hand, your curiosity is aroused and you decide to investigate further, then you will be doing exactly what was done between 1927 and 1932 by a new team of investigators headed by Elton Mayo, Fritz Roethlisberger, and William Dickson.[1]

Let us assume that you, like the Mayo team, choose to investigate further. You set up a new experiment, this time with a group of employees who assemble telephone relays. You are still concerned with how variations in the working conditions can influence employee productivity on the job. So now you vary several factors and observe what happens. Here is what you discover:

1. You institute rest periods of various durations. Result: Productivity goes up.
2. You provide soup and a sandwich on the job. Result: Productivity goes up.
3. You shorten the workday by an hour. Result: Productivity goes up.

1. E. Mayo, F. Roethlisberger, and W. Dickson, *Management and the Worker,* Harvard University Press, Cambridge, Mass., 1939.

How do you explain your findings? You might reasonably surmise that rest periods, refreshments, and a shorter workday are highly conducive to productivity. If you do, in fact, subscribe to such an explanation, then you might be a bit hard-pressed to account for this additional experimental finding:

4. For three months all rest periods, refreshments and shortened working days are eliminated, and the employees return to the work schedule they followed before the experiment began. Result: Productivity reaches a new high—and stays there during the entire 12 weeks.

What *is* going on here? And if that's not enough to raise havoc with your scientific theories, consider the final investigative result:

5. Rest periods and refreshments are reintroduced Result: Output climbs higher still.

O.K., scientist—what's the verdict? It seems that no matter what changes you introduce, worker output increases. Why? Elton Mayo and his associates were faced with the same question over a half century ago when they actually conducted the study with the employees who assembled telephone relays in the Hawthorne Division of the Western Electric Company. They came up with the findings I just described.

How did the Mayo team explain the results? First, they realized that something more than changed working conditions were influencing worker productivity on the job. Then they identified what that "something more" was: the *human dimension*—the social and psychological condition of the employees in the workplace. The results of the Hawthorne studies seemed to indicate that the employees were more satisfied and worked harder because Mayo and his associates were *paying attention* to them, making them feel more worthwhile and important on the job. By creating changes in the workplace, the Mayo team was altering the *physical* environment; but more important as far as productivity was concerned, it was also transforming the *psychological* environment by fulfilling the social and personal needs of the workers.

Now, did you guess that it was the human element producing all those strange results at the Hawthorne plant of Western Electric? If you didn't, don't feel bad—neither did Mayo and his colleagues when they first puzzled over their unexpected experimental results. In fact, it took 5 years of experimentation with over 20,000 employee-subjects before they were reasonable sure of what exactly *was* accounting for the increases in productivity.

We all owe a debt of sorts to Mayo and his associates. Even though their work has received some critical brickbats among the bouquets, they were responsible for focusing managerial attention on the human dimension in the workplace. They were also among the first behavioral scientists to recognize that workers can be motivated by social and psychological (as well as economic) needs.

Using Rewards to Pay Attention to the Worker

The Mayo team discovered the importance of paying attention to the worker, how it could increase employee output and satisfaction at the same time. Their discovery remains relevant today. In fact, as I pointed out in the previous chapter, paying attention to the worker is basic to determining worker needs and practicing effective behavior modification.

On the following pages I will be discussing fourteen different rewards you can use in satisfying your employees' needs and encouraging their productivity. These rewards are:

1. Praise
   a. Job-relevant
   b. Non-job-relevant
2. Public recognition
3. Job security
4. Money
5. Fringe benefits
6. Employee development programs
   a. Job enrichment
   b. Personality (and leadership) development
   c. Mental and physical health
7. Employee involvement in decision making
8. Leisure time
9. Feedback
10. Social participation
11. Company spirit (pride)
12. Opportunity to achieve and advance in the organization
13. Degrees of freedom at work
14. Pleasant forms of moderate distraction

Every time you administer a reward you are, in effect, paying attention to the worker; your goal will be to give your subordinates those rewards that best satisfy their particular needs. In other words, you want to achieve a match between workers' needs and the rewards they receive on the job.

Before I turn to a discussion of the various rewards, I will list some points that should help you choose and administer your rewards more effectively. A more complete discussion of these points will be found in Chapter 8.

1. Most of the fourteen rewards are geared to satisfying social, esteem, or self-fulfillment needs. This reflects our thinking that most contemporary workers have needs that fall in the upper ranges of the Maslow hierarchy.
2. The reward that works best is the reward that satisfies a worker's need(s) most successfully.
3. Many workers have several different needs at once, allowing you to use several different kinds of rewards in such circumstances.
4. Certain rewards can satisfy more than one human need. That is, some rewards overlap need levels in the Maslow hierarchy (for instance, money can satisfy physiological, safety, and esteem needs).
5. Certain needs can be satisfied by more than one reward. Choose the reward that works best for the individual worker in question.
6. Be on the lookout for boredom effects if you use the same reward frequently for a particular employee.
7. Don't be afraid to experiment with using the various rewards. The more rewards you can utilize effectively, the better manager you'll be.

Reward 1: Praise

There are two kinds of praise you can use to satisfy worker needs: *job-relevant* praise and *non-job-relevant* praise. Let me discuss each in turn.

Job-Relevant Praise

Complimenting a worker for a job well done is probably the simplest and most basic reward you can administer—and it is also one of the most effective. Remember the survey in Chapter 5? Number 1 on the workers' "want parade" was full appreciation of work done. Praising an employee for superior job performance can show that appreciation, and unlike some rewards, such as money, it doesn't cost you anything.

Management professor and author Dr. Michael LeBoeuf had this to say when asked if praise pays with today's employees: "There are two things people want more than sex and money . . . recognition and praise."[2] That is a pretty powerful statement . . . and while some skeptics might challenge it, praise and recognition for good workplace behavior *does* enhance employee satisfaction and productivity.

With all the benefits accruing from the use of praise, you'd think that contemporary managers would use it frequently. Right?

Wrong! Very few managers use praise or use it often enough; in fact, some are stingier with compliments than Scrooge was with money. Managers who have his attitude toward praise can usually be classified into one of three types. If you've ever had a job, you'll probably think I knew some of the managers you worked for.

Type 1: The Negativistic Manager This is the type of person who seems to have mastered the now-you-see-him, now-you-don't routine. You see him when things go wrong, and you don't when things go right. Here's how one employee described the behavior of her negativistic manager:

> I work in sales at a large department store, and my manager has plenty of opportunity to observe my performance. On Monday I came to work and had a very good morning. My manager said nothing. Monday afternoon I sold about normal, and still my manager said nothing. On Tuesday I had an exceptional day: I sold way over average. My manager said nothing. On Wednesday I had an average sales morning and a good afternoon. My manager said nothing. Thursday I got to work a bit early for the storewide sale and put in a busy, high-sales day. My manager said nothing. Friday started O.K., I sold about normal. My manager said nothing. Then at 2:15 Friday afternoon I made a mistake that lost us a sale. Bam! The ceiling fell in. From out of nowhere the manager came racing up and began hounding me about losing the sale. *All I'd like to know is where the hell was she all week long when I was doing great?*

The negativistic manager is the person responsible for the often-heard worker lament: The only time my manager talks with me about my work is when I do something wrong. Is it any wonder the worker gripes? The negativistic manager is a real motivation-destroyer. Nobody likes to feel that good work is ignored while any mistake receives maximum management attention. As one worker so aptly told her manager: "At least if you're going to criticize my mistakes, give equal time to my successes."

Type 2: The Perfectionistic Manager This type of person isn't unwilling to praise a worker for a job well done *as long as the job is done perfectly*. The problem is, the perfectionistic

2. M. LeBoeuf, *The Greatest Management Principle in the World*, Putnam Publishing Group, New York, 1985.

manager's standards are so high that hardly anybody reaches the competence level required to trigger a kind word.

I have had many perfectionistic managers approach me and ask, "Why should I praise workers if they don't measure up to my standard of excellence? Didn't you say that praise should be given only when you think a person honestly deserves it?"

My answers to such inquiries are always the same. Yes, you should only praise a worker when you can do so honestly, but there are ways you can honestly praise a person for work not yet up to your standards while, at the same time, encouraging that person to reach those high standards in the future. Here is what you do. Note the employee's work performance over a period of time. You will see that it varies; that is, sometimes it is better than other times. Now it might be true that even when the worker is performing best, the work might not measure up to your standards; but that shouldn't stop you from congratulating the worker for a better work performance.

There is a difference between saying, "Hey, Ms. Jones, I want to congratulate you on doing better" and "Hey, Ms. Jones, you're doing great work." Possibly, by rewarding a worker for an improvement in work performance you'll encourage that worker to keep improving until reaching, someday, a level a competence that justifies compliments without qualifications. (By the way, rewarding a worker for performance that approaches an ideal standard is called reinforcement by "successive approximations" and is an effective way to increase worker performance and satisfaction on the job.)

Make sure you don't get trapped in the pitfalls of either negativistic or perfectionistic managing when it's your turn to step into a supervisory role. Be prepared to use praise as an effective reward for deserving employees, particularly when those employees have either social or esteem needs, or both.

There are many ways to give praise on the job . . . but no matter how it is administered it should always be (1) honest (the employee should deserve the praise), (2) fair (everyone should have an equal chance of getting praise for similar performance), and (3) not so frequent that it loses its effectiveness. When an employee's performance is so great that you feel too much praise might become a problem, then alternate praise with one or more of the other rewards in this chapter. That should help reduce the danger of any one reward losing its potency through overuse.

Now, before we leave the topic of job relevant praise, let me introduce one final "type" of manager who can sap the motivation and personal satisfaction of even the most dedicated employee. I call this individual. . .

Type 3: The Sadistic Manager Managers of this type freely give praise and recognition to employees so—on the surface—they seem fine. But wait! These managers have a unique way of balancing their words of praise and criticism when it comes to assessing their employees. And the rule of thumb seems to be this: employees can accumulate as many incidents of praise as their behavior warrants; yet, if they do something that calls for criticism then that one error/mistake "wipes out" all (or most of) the praise "earned" along the way. It would be like having a bank account where you could make as many deposits as you liked . . . but one withdrawal from the account automatically reverted your total balance back to zero.

Such an approach, of course, can have devastating effects on employees. One production worker put it this way: "What good are all my supervisors compliments when I know that one mistake can wipe them out. I'm always waiting for the other shoe to fall. I'd rather not have any praise at all."

Is it any wonder I have chosen to label this type of manager "sadistic?" Even though the manager might not always realize what he/she is doing (or the negative impact it has), such inappropriate behavior must be curtailed if a worthplace is to be created.

The Negativistic Manager. The Perfectionistic Manager. The Sadistic Manager. Three types of manager you don't want to be. When it's your turn to create the worthplace and oversee the actions of subordinates, remember these three messages:

1. *To the Negativistic manager who would choose not to praise:* It is appropriate to criticize an individual for poor performance, however it is also appropriate to praise an individual for good performance. There should be a balance.
2. *To the Perfectionistic manager who would set standards for praise too high:* It is reasonable to expect competent performance . . . but unreasonable to set standards so high that they are unreachable. The goal of management should be to set challenging, achievable goals for employees . . . and recognize subordinates for progress made toward realizing those goals.
3. *To the Sadistic manager who would offer praise with a "string" attached:* There must be some level of "equity" between the weighing of good vs not-so-good performance and a recognition that accumulated incidents of positive job behavior should not be rendered worthless because of one (non-critical) mistake.

Non-Job-Relevant Praise

Praise, to be effective, doesn't have to be limited to job performance. People like to be complimented on a whole range of behaviors, and that is where non-job-relevant praise comes in.

Let us presume that you're a manager, and one day you spot a subordinate walking into the office wearing a new outfit. If you honestly think the clothes are attractive, why not compliment the employee for having good taste? Such praise accomplishes two things:

1. It clearly demonstrates to your employees that you are aware of them (many workers complain that their supervisors don't even know who they are).
2. It satisfies the workers' need for social approval or external validation of their personal worth or for both.

There are many instances in which you as a manager will have the opportunity to practice non-job-relevant praise. For example:

1. Changes in a worker's personal appearance you find suitable for praise
2. Acquisitions by a worker (for instance, a new car, house, briefcase, or watch) you find suitable for praise
3. Significant occasions in a worker's life (for example, birthday, weddings, graduations)
4. Significant off-the-job achievements in a worker's life (for instance, civic awards, election to office in a social or fraternal organization, religious activities, outstanding performance in sports)

Normally, workers are proud of their non-job-relevant activities, and they will be pleased that you chose to share their pride; however, let me make a few cautionary recommendations:

1. Some workers feel strongly about keeping their work life and personal life separate. Thus, they may feel offended by a manager who invades the privacy of their off-the-job world. This is a relatively rare problem, but one you should keep in mind when giving out non-job-relevant praise.
2. If you are going to congratulate one worker on a special occasion (birthday, graduation, marriage, or other occasion), then you should acknowledge every other worker when similar events occur. The only way you can do this is to gather information from the same source(s) and to be sure to do so regularly.
3. Most workers are pleased to be remembered for positive, happy occasions but might be miffed if a manager was to bring up a negative, I'd-like-to-forget-the-whole-thing event. For example, it would be the height of bad taste for you as a manager to send your employee a note congratulating him for beating a drunken driving rap.

This brings us to a sensitive issue. What should a manager do about an employee's personal tragedy, for instance, a death in the immediate family? There is no general rule I can give you to cover that kind of situation, except possibly to warn you to handle each incident with great tact and care. Under normal circumstances I see no reason why a condolence card cannot be sent, or possibly flowers or a contribution according to the wishes set forth in the obituary. I also feel it is within the bounds of good taste to express your sympathy upon the employee's return to work and your willingness to be of help should any help be desired. An employee will normally appreciate such a considerate gesture and show appreciation in on-the-job performance.

Reward 2: Public Recognition

One of my friends is an engineer with an interesting story to tell. It seems that a few years back he was working at a large company that combined public recognition with employee parking in a unique fashion. Here is what happened.

At the particular company parking was a problem, with employee lots strung out a good distance from the main plant. In fact, some of the outlying parking spaces were a 20-minute walk away, which meant that closer-in parking was coveted by all the workers. Then there were six assigned parking places as close-in as one could get, three on either side of the main plant door, where all employees entered the building. Five of the six slots were reserved for company officers, and each bore the name of the particular executive painted on a large wooden sign. And the sixth space?

It was reserved for the "employee of the month," complete with name painted in bold letters on the parking sign nearby. The benefits of such an honor were clear to the winners: (1) they saved up to 40 minutes a day walking to and from their cars; (2) they got the opportunity to "rub shoulders" with top company officials every day; and (3) all employees walking into the plant saw the name of the employee of the month.

Now that's public recognition! Of course, such recognition doesn't have to be so elaborate to be effective—for instance, simply praising a person in front of others is a form of public recognition that can be very successful. What makes public recognition effective is sharing the news of a worker's meritorious service with others. Individuals with social and esteem needs want the approval of their supervisors and their peers; they want the external validation of their worth that leads to a sense of self-respect and personal pride. And they get it through public recognition.

There are many ways you can give public recognition on the job, some of which you may already be familiar with.

1. Employee of the month. This is one of the most common forms of public recognition and can be utilized for any number of reasons (for example, highest sales, best suggestion, least absenteeism, highest output, least errors).
2. Secretary for a day. This is normally a promotion sponsored by radio stations. The winner is publicly recognized over the air and often gets a packet of treats (such as dinner and gift certificates) as well. Normally, managers nominate their own secretaries for the contest.
3. Million-dollar round table or similar types of "clubs." Here, people are publicly recognized for achieving significant sales in a calendar year. Often insurance companies will publish pictures of their million-dollar round-table representatives in a periodical like *Time*. Not only does this reward the employee, it also affords him/her the opportunity to cut the picture out and have it framed for the office, where customers will be duly impressed.
4. Write-ups in the company periodical or the local newspaper.
5. Public praise.
6. Various performance charts or posters showing how an employee is doing on the job. (Sometimes performance charts or posters are used to show sales or other work indices as part of company contests.)
7. Administering honors or awards. Some companies have annual banquets where top employees receive special gifts or praise for superior performances.
8. Change in job title.
9. Publicly announced merit raises or bonuses.
10. Bestowing status symbols when appropriate.

The topic of status deserves special mention. There is a whole range of items that can be given to employees for superior performance, some of which are recognized by those employees and their coworkers as *status symbols*. What is recognized as a status symbol can vary from company to company and person to person; yet, some items seem to be almost universally recognized as status-relevant. Normally, we say something is a status symbol when (1) people want it, (2) not everyone can have it, and (3) possession of it gives the owner a degree of prestige.

In the business world there are many generally recognized status symbols, ranging all the way from the old favorite, the executive washroom key, to the ever popular company car, bigger desk, and larger office.[3] Remember almost anything can become a status symbol if it is recognized in those terms by the workers in the company.[4]

Using public recognition as a reward can be very effective in motivating workers and satisfying their needs, particularly if those needs are in the social and esteem range of the Maslow hierarchy. But certain precautions must be taken lest such rewards lead to serious difficulties.

3. Speaking of nicer offices, I had an interesting experience with this type of status symbol at the university. The building where I worked had two kinds of offices: windowed outer offices and windowless inner offices. One of my students pointed out that he thought the more desirable windowed offices were status symbols given out to professors of the highest rank. I checked out the hypothesis, and sure enough, almost every windowed office was occupied by a full professor, whereas the inner offices were assigned to faculty of lower ranks (associate and assistant professors).

4. Whenever you give a worker some special privilege or equipment be aware that other workers might perceive this as a status symbol—even if you don't intend it that way. A few years ago a telephone company installer was replacing phones in the secretarial pool. The order called for several dozen black phones, one per desk—all in plain view of every other desk in the room. Unfortunately, the installer ended up one black phone short. "No problem," he muttered. He took a yellow phone from the truck and put it on the last desk. By noontime the next day there was almost a general strike by the secretaries who were enraged that one of their colleagues had gotten a yellow phone—a status symbol she didn't "deserve."

1. When giving public recognition, do it fairly across the board; in other words, don't play favorites. Every employee should have an equal chance to gain public recognition for work performed.
2. Be wary of possible conflict between workers over public recognition. Particularly in small businesses you must be sure that public recognition doesn't stir up jealousies or destructive rivalries between employees.
3. Be concerned if one employee gets a disproportionate share of public recognition. Not only can this lead to distress, frustration, and even "giving up" in other workers; it can also cause public recognition to lose its effectiveness for the recipient when it is over-used or, worse, when the recipient shuns it to avoid rejection by the "overlooked" coworkers.
4. Most employees welcome public recognition, but some are shy about being placed in the limelight. If you have subordinates who feel uncomfortable in the glare of public attention, use other rewards to motivate them.

Reward 3: Job Security

As somebody who has battled for academic tenure, the issue of job security is dear to my heart. It's dear to the hearts of labor union representatives, too, and they have repeatedly struggled to gain contractual recognition of job security for workers.

From our earlier discussion it is evident that job security is not the motivator it once was. This is partially due to the fact that many contemporary workers already *have* that security. Then, too, until recently jobs were relatively abundant, and people could find employment if they were willing to look for it. Finally, with the advent of social legislation (for instance, unemployment compensation and welfare) people realized that being out of a job didn't mean being out of a meal. How vital is job security when the unemployed can depend on governmental programs to satisfy their basic needs? (This is particularly true for low-income workers, who can sometimes make more on welfare than on a job.)

Of course, should the economic picture turn bleak (high unemployment, tight money, and so forth), then the reward value of job security will increase once again. Thus your decision to use job security as a reinforcement will hinge, in part, on your reading of current economic conditions. Here are some other factors you'll want to consider when contemplating the use of job security:

1. The reward of job security is most appreciated by individuals who are lower on the Maslow hierarchy, particularly those with *safety* needs.
2. Job security as a reward will be most effective in industries hit hardest by unemployment and economic turmoil (for instance, at the beginning of the 1980s job security became a big issue to workers in the automobile industry).
3. Job security works least effectively for workers who are highly competent or have marketable skills, as they know they will have an easier time finding another job should the need arise.
4. In some companies, job security is already guaranteed in the employment contract, at which point it ceases to be an effective reward
5. If you satisfy a worker's safety need by giving job security, recognize that new needs will predominate and change your rewards accordingly.

6. The need for job security tends to be highest when people get older (it's not as easy to find another job at an advanced age) and when they experience an upsurge in financial obligations (such as young children and unexpected bills).

Reward 4: Money

With all this talk about workers' "higher needs" and the importance of psychological rewards, some of you might think I'm down on good old-fashioned money as an effective reinforcement. Nothing could be further from the truth. Money is still a very basic consideration in any jobholders' mind, and at least one management authority believes: "Money may not be the only people motivator, but many realists believe it's still the strongest one around. Apart from the material things, money buys education and opportunity, peace of mind, dignity, and more. In large measure, if you know what to do with it money buys happiness."[5]

The same author recognizes, however, that money is not "the *only* motivator—people respond as well to interesting and meaningful work, humane treatment, or a feeling of importance and belonging."[6] In other words, there's more to life than cash.

When is it best to use money as a motivator on the job? When your employees require it to satisfy either physiological or safety needs or both. In general, workers who have financial hardships (because of unexpected costs, additional expenses, downturns in the economy, or low wages) find money more rewarding than employees who are more financially secure. There is however, an exception to this rule. Some people equate money with self-worth and attempt to accumulate as much as they can to satisfy their esteem needs. For them, money is always a valuable reward, no matter how much they get.

Money can also be an effective motivator when it is given in a way that satisfies more than one need at a time. For example, a merit raise, publicly announced, can satisfy lower-*and* higher-level needs simultaneously.

Finally, money rewards are often effective with part-time employees, particularly those who don't see their part-time job leading to full-time employment. Part-time employees often take work *specifically* to make money and, lacking any long-term commitment to the job, are not as excited by rewards that appeal to the career needs of full-time employees. It's like the difference one sees between a house renter and a house buyer. The person who buys a house sees it as a long-term investment and takes pride in that investment. A renter, on the other hand, has no such long-term commitment to the house and often treats it differently for that reason.

What are the problems with using money as a reward? There are two basic difficulties:

1. In most cases, if you use it too often or give out too much, it tends to lose some of its reinforcing effectiveness (even a starving person can get too much to eat).
2. Many times your financial resources will be limited, and you won't have funds available to use as rewards. In these circumstances it is imperative that you have other rewards ready for use with your employees.

5. Cited in M. Karlins, "International Approaches to Productivity Management: The Singapore Experience", Paper presented at the Eastern Regional Convention of AHRMOB, May 7, 1986, p. 6.
6. Ibid.

In summary, money can be an effective reward, but it's not the *only* effective reward, and it shouldn't be used exclusively to increase worker productivity and satisfaction on the job. Remember, man does not live by bread alone.

Reward 5: Fringe Benefits

There are numerous kinds of fringe benefits employees can receive on the job—and, like money, how they are presented will determine what needs they can fulfill. In general, fringe benefits help satisfy safety (security) needs; but when they are tangible objects like company cars, then they can act as status symbols or a form of public recognition which can lead to satisfaction of esteem needs.

When asked if fringe benefits play a role in motivating workers, management adviser Arthur Witkin had this to say:

> Some recent studies show that fringes, when absent, can serve to demotivate, but when they're present, they aren't a positive motivating force. . . Many psychologists, including myself, have accepted the fact that there are so-called hygienic factors involved in job satisfaction. If those factors aren't there, the company's in trouble because workers will feel their absence. But to pile on more of them has no noticeable effect in making workers more satisfied or more productive.[7]

This is an interesting point of view and seems to suggest that a certain number of fringe benefits are necessary because employees expect them, but that beyond that number they don't have much motivational impact. The vital question becomes: How *many* fringe benefits does the employee expect? There is no easy answer to this inquiry, as different workers in different industries have different needs and expectations.

In today's business world, most workers have come to expect fringe benefits like vacations, sick leave, and good group health insurance; beyond that, however, you will have to test and see whether additional benefits are worth the cost in terms of increased satisfaction and productivity in your employees.

Reward 6: Employee Development Programs

There are three kinds of employee development programs you can use to satisfy worker needs: (1) job enrichment, (2) personality (and leadership) development, and (3) mental and physical health. Let me discuss each in turn.

Job Enrichment

Let me introduce this topic with a personal story. A few years ago I was on a promotional tour, appearing on various radio and television programs to discuss a book I had written. Most of these programs were talk shows, involving 10 to 15 minutes of discussion between the host and myself. It was a comfortable, easygoing format. There was one exception, however: Somehow I had been scheduled to discuss my book on a morning rock show—the kind with a disc jockey who plays "Top Ten" music to legions of rock fans listening frenetically by their radios. The idea of discussing my book between hit records, weather reports, and local ad spots—all at the hyperspeed

7. A. Witkin (interview), "How Bosses Get People to Work Harder," *U.S. News & World Report,* Jan. 29, 1979, p. 64.

preferred by disc jockeys—was a trifle disconcerting, but I knew it would be worth it. You see, most of my youth was spent dreaming about becoming a disc jockey, and now, at last, I was going to meet one face to face.

And I wasn't disappointed—at least, not at first. In fact, I was so fascinated with the disc jockey and his control room antics that I hardly remember the actual program. Afterward he invited me to lunch in the station's cafeteria. I gladly accepted. We ate at a small table by ourselves, and I waited patiently until he was finished before I asked him *the* question.

"Tell me," I asked, "How does it feel?"

He looked at me blankly. "What do you mean?"

"How does it *really* feel to be a disc jockey?"

His expression didn't change.

I decided to elaborate. "I mean, how does it feel to be right in the center of things—with rock stars on the one side, and the fans on the other . . . and you right in the middle of the action?"

The disc jockey—my hero—stared straight ahead with tired eyes and shattered my little illusion with one verbal shot. "It feels boring," he said flatly, "all I want to do is go home and go sailing." And with that he nodded goodbye and walked out of the cafeteria.

I sat stunned for several minutes before I got up and headed for the exit. On my way out I passed an observation window where I could see the afternoon disc jockey spinning records and talking into his microphone. I stopped to watch his frantic activity and then it hit me: Yes, it would be great to be a disc jockey for a while—a year, maybe two—but then how interesting would it be to sit in a little cubicle and tout the local pizza palace while spinning little discs on a turntable and making the weather sound as exciting as the play by play of the superbowl? Not very exciting at all, I decided, and I began to understand what my host had meant about boredom a few minutes before.

You know, boredom is a very important factor in the human condition. It can motivate us to expand our horizons as we seek new kinds of stimulation; yet, it can also be the "rust of human emotion," leading to dissatisfaction with people, jobs, and activities as we become used to them.

Let us consider boredom and its relationship to work. Any job, no matter what kind it is, has the potential to become boring to the jobholder if the job remains basically the same over a long period of time. This is because, as we learn a job, the skills that were once a challenge become automatic, and the things that were novel and exciting when we started work become mundane and predictable after being repeated day after day.

How *fast* a job becomes boring will vary, depending in part on the complexity of the job, how much the job changes over time, the personality of the employee, and the skills of the manager in keeping the employee satisfied and productive. (I have often heard a worker comment: "I'd quit this boring job if it wasn't for my manager.")

Only recently have behavioral scientists begun to recognize the significance of boredom in affecting worker satisfaction and productivity. To combat this motivation crippler they have come up with an antidote: *job enrichment.* They have studied the effectiveness of this antidote in the workplace, usually on the assembly line type of job, where the repetitive, relatively simple kinds of tasks invite boredom.

Do not think, however, that the assembly line is the only place where boredom can strike with devastating results. Remember *any* job can get boring if a person stays on it long enough and the job doesn't change. And that goes for blue-collar work, white-collar work, unskilled labor, professional work, and—yes—managerial work, too.

As a manager what can you do about boredom? How can you combat this potentially destructive factor and keep worker satisfaction and productivity high? By utilizing job enrichment when possible—that is, when your efforts are allowed by upper management and existing contractual obligations.[8] Here are two objectives you'll want to accomplish in overcoming boredom.

Objective 1: Identify Bored Workers Not all workers are bored with their jobs. You'll have to determine which ones are bored before you can take corrective action. (Trying to modify the work conditions of a person who is *not* bored on the job can create a terrible hassle.) If a worker has been assigned a specific job for a long time, and if that job is relatively easy for the particular worker to master, then the possibility of boredom increases. Watch for telltale signs, such as listlessness and lack of interest at work, increasing complaints and absenteeism, and loss of morale and productivity. Of course, these signs can also be indications of problems other than boredom—and if they remain after Objective 2 is attempted, then you'll want to look for other causes of the worker's dissatisfaction.

Objective 2: Help Workers Overcome Their Boredom through Job Enrichment There are several ways you as a manager can help workers enrich their work world. The best way is to expand job responsibilities at a rate which keeps the employee challenged but not overwhelmed. Thus, as a person masters job skills, additional or different ones are assigned. Sometimes this means expanding a specific job to include new responsibilities and skills; other times it means promoting an employee to a new job "up the line." In either case, the emphasis is on giving the employee job enrichment to maintain interest and fend off boredom in the workplace.

"But," some of you may be asking, "what if an employee doesn't want new responsibilities? What if that person is happy the way things are?"

These are reasonable questions and deserve careful answers. Let me deal with the second question first: If the worker *is* happy the way things are, then my recommendation is to "let sleeping dogs lie"—don't tamper with an employee's job if he likes it the way it is. Normally, happy workers are *not* bored workers; they are usually interested, satisfied, and productive in the workplace—which means that you, the manager, will have reason to be happy, too.

Now, for the first question, there will probably be some workers who are bored and do not want new or additional responsibilities. You will have to use your best judgment as to whether forcing changes on these workers will later be met with a "Thank you, I wish you had done that earlier" or with even greater dissatisfaction on the job. Fortunately, you won't have to make this judgment very often, because in most cases bored workers welcome a chance to get out of their rut into work that is more challenging and stimulating.

Boredom is not an enjoyable human condition—people normally strive to avoid or eliminate it. If you can help them in their quest, all the better for you and for the worker. Just make sure that the workers don't feel you're ripping them off in the process. A worker who might readily take on new job challenges as a means of overcoming boredom may pass up the chance completely if that worker senses the manager is merely trying to get more work without paying for it. The best way to approach the idea of job enrichment, then, is in a voluntary context—giving the worker the option to accept or reject the job opportunities. That way, the employee will see the offer in the positive way it was intended, rather than as simply another attempt to get more work at no extra pay.

There are numerous job enrichment programs you can utilize with your employees. Some require additional education or training programs, which in themselves help combat boredom. Here are some job enrichment approaches you can use to help combat boredom on the job. Whichever

---

8. Sometimes upper management or the employee contract (or both) very specifically limits the degree to which a job can be expanded. Be sure you know how much you can change a person's job before you start a job enrichment program with your employees.

ones you choose should be adapted to your particular work circumstances for maximum effectiveness.

1. On some jobs (for instance, on assembly lines) it is possible to rotate workers through several types of jobs, thus relieving the boredom of doing the same task time after time.
2. You can continually expand a person's job to encompass new skills and responsibilities.
3. You can promote an individual to a new job that may be more demanding.
4. You can change a person's working environment, to keep it novel and stimulating (see Reward 14).
5. You can let the worker get involved in team production efforts (see Reward 10).
6. You can give the worker more "degrees of freedom" in controlling the job (see Reward 13).
7. You can let the worker participate in the managerial decision-making process (see Reward 7).

Before moving on to the other forms of employee development programs, let me make one final point about job enrichment.

It is sometimes tempting to look at certain kinds of jobs—particularly repetitive ones like those on assembly lines—and automatically label them boring. This is a bad mistake you shouldn't make. A job that seems boring to one person might be perfectly satisfying and even highly challenging to someone else; it will depend to a great degree on the ability of the person to perform the task in question. There are always some individuals who enjoy doing the very jobs that others would find boring the minute they walk in the door.

As a manager, you should be striving for successful job-worker matches—in other words, jobs that fit the needs of the individual workers performing them. In doing this, don't ask yourself, "Would I find this job boring?"; ask yourself, rather, "Would my employee find this job boring?" After all, it's the worker who is going to have to do the work.

Personality (and Leadership) Development

Almost all major corporations and many smaller businesses offer their employees the opportunity to attend various seminars and workshops designed to improve job performance through the development of personal strengths (for example, creativity development and assertiveness training). These programs can run from a few hours to a full week of intensive "marathon" sessions, and they are normally conducted by in-house specialists (usually the organizational development staff) or outside consultants hired for training purposes.

Because personality and leadership development programs normally require the direction of specialists, you probably won't be called upon to conduct any workshops unless you've had specialized training to do so. Therefore, I simply call these programs to your attention as another approach to improving worker satisfaction and productivity on the job. If your particular company doesn't have such programs, you might want to recommend their implementation—if you think they would be of value in your particular work environment.

Mental and Physical Health Programs

American business is waking to the profound personal and financial waste that occurs when a valued employee is mentally or physically incapacitated at the height of a productive career. In many cases, such mental or physical breakdowns could have been prevented had the proper preventative steps been taken. Major American corporations are now committed to developing programs to help safeguard the health and mental well-being of their employees.

Most employee development programs share a common characteristic—they are rewarding because they make workers feel better about themselves. This "feeling better" can take many forms. Sometimes a worker feels more enthusiastic and less bored with life (job enrichment), other times more self-confident (personality development) or robust and alert (physical health). Whatever form it takes, however, can be rewarding to the individual, and for that reason employee development programs provide an effective method for increasing worker satisfaction and productivity on the job.

Reward 7: Employee Involvement In Decision Making

The following incident took place many years ago in a company that manufactured wooden toys. One part of the process consisted of spraying paint on partially assembled toys, and then hanging them on an overhead belt of continuously moving hooks which carried the toys into a drying oven. The eight employees who did the painting sat in a line in front of the hooks. The plant engineers had calculated the speed of the belt so that a trained employee would be able to hang a freshly painted toy on each hook before it passed out of reach. The employees were paid on a piece rate basis, determined by their performance as a group. New employees were put on a learning bonus, which decreased every month. At the end of 6 months, the learning bonus was cut off and the employees were on their own.

The painting operation was a management headache. High turnover, low morale, and frequent absenteeism were the symptoms. The employees complained that the hooks were moving too fast and that the time study engineers had set the piece rates wrong. Many of the hooks were moving into the oven without toys on them.

A consultant was hired by the plant management to study the situation. After preliminary investigation, the consultant tried several times to persuade the supervisor to call a meeting of the toy painters to discuss working conditions with them. The reluctant supervisor finally agreed, and the first of several meetings was held right after the end of a shift. At the meeting a spokesperson for the employees elaborated on their complaints about the speed of the hooks. She explained that they could keep up with the moving hooks for short periods of time but purposely held back for fear that they would be expected to maintain the pace all day long. What they wanted was to "adjust the speed of the belt faster or slower, depending on how we feel." The supervisor agreed to pass this request along to the engineers and superintendent.

As might be expected, the engineers reacted unfavorably to the proposal, and only after much persuasion did they agree to try out the idea. The supervisor had a graduated control dial with points marked low, medium, and fast installed at the booth of one of the employees. The speed of the belt could now be adjusted within these limits.

What happened? The toy painters were delighted with this arrangement and spent much of their free time during the first few days deciding how the speed of the belt should be varied from time to time during the day. Within a week the pattern had been established. The productivity of the group as well as their morale went up considerably. The quality of their work was as satisfactory as it had been previously. And it is interesting to note that the average speed at which the toy painters were running the belt was *higher* than the constant speed they had been complaining about to the supervisor.

For our purposes, the true story of the toy painters illustrates an extremely important principle for effective managing. If you want to increase worker satisfaction and productivity on the job, then involve your employees in the managerial decision-making process.

In the toy factory, the employees were given the opportunity to become involved in the decision-making process. They made recommendations about how the conveyor belt should move, and those recommendations were followed. What happened? Worker satisfaction and productivity increased.

The toy factory results are not unique. In fact, the value of employee involvement in decision making (also referred to as "participative management" in some circles) is one of the most documented and replicated findings in all behavioral science.

By involving your employees in the decision-making process, three benefits can result:

1. Workers who play an active role in the decision-making process will be more likely to go along with whatever decision is reached.
2. Workers who play an active role in the decision-making process will carry out those decisions in a more enthusiastic, motivated manner.
3. By involving your workers in the decision-making process you increase your chances of finding the best possible solution to any given problem. (This is because an employee may come up with a solution which is better than any you were able to devise.)

Many contemporary managers balk at the suggestion that they involve their workers in the decision-making process. They usually base their opposition on arguments that fall apart when held up to close scrutiny. Let me present these arguments and reveal why you as a manager don't have to worry about them if you decide to use employee involvement in decision making as a reward in the workplace.

Argument 1 I can't let my employees share in decision making because they might come up with a recommendation I can't live with.

My Response Involving employees in the decision-making process doesn't mean that you have to accept every recommendation they make. There are times when your employees will come up with the same recommendation you favor or with a suggestion that you think is better than your own. In such cases you can use their inputs. Other times they won't have any ideas on the problem or their suggestions will be unacceptable (or inferior to your own). In those cases, thank your subordinates for their assistance and go with your own best suggestion.

Argument 2 I can't let my employees share in decision making because if I reject their recommendations they'll become frustrated and demotivated on the job.

My Response Not necessarily so. If you consistently ask employees for their suggestions and never use any of them, or if you accept employee suggestions on minor issues and ignore them on every major problem that comes along, then you might have a problem with employee morale. On the other hand, no employees expect a manager to accept every suggestion they make; in fact, they might question your managerial competence if you did. As long as your subordinates feel you are asking for their help in good faith—accepting suggestions which are appropriate and rejecting those which are not—you'll be in good shape.

Argument 3 I don't want to involve my employees in decision making, because then I'll have to check with them every time a problem comes up.

My Response This isn't true. You can involve your employees in decision making as often or as little as you want. There will be some times and problems where soliciting employee inputs will be irrelevant or inappropriate. Also, situations will arise where there is not time to consult with subordinates or where subordinates have no desire to be involved in the decision-making process. Don't let such instances hassle you. Involve your employees when you think it will increase their satisfaction and productivity on the job.

Argument 4 I don't want to involve my employees in decision making because they aren't capable of making decisions.

My Response Often employees are more capable of assisting in decision making than managers realize. This is not because they are brighter than managers, but, rather, because they can bring different perspectives to bear on the problem in question. Let me give you an example. During World War II, an Allied airbase in the Pacific was having supply problems. One item in short supply was protective glass encasements for the landing lights. The ranking officer on the base was at a loss to solve the problem, so he decided to solicit recommendations from base personnel. Within a few hours the problem was solved. A cook in the mess hall, hearing of the problem, quickly realized that empty peanut butter jars would fit perfectly over the landing lights. Not only did the jars fit as well as the original encasements, but they were also stronger and withstood more pounding before breaking. Who would have figured a cook could solve a problem a base commander couldn't crack? The reason he could was that he brought a different perspective to the problem. He worked with peanut butter jars every day, the commanding officer did not. Remember, don't sell your employees short when it comes to giving aid in problem solving. More and more companies are realizing that when it comes to solving work problems, who should know better than the people who do the work.

Argument 5 I can't let my employees share in decision making because decision making is my job as a manager.

My Response It is your job to make decisions, but that doesn't mean you can't have help. Remember, by involving your employees in the decision-making process you gain additional input for solving the problem. You also create more motivated, satisfied, and productive workers—and that's your job as a manager, too.

Argument 6 I can't let my employees share in decision making because they'll think I'm incompetent and can't solve problems on my own.

My Response If you sat quietly by and let your employees solve every problem that came along, maybe this would be a possibility. If, however, you get actively involved in the decision-making process, sharing your ideas with your employees and vice versa, then you will not be seen as incompetent but, rather, a concerned manager who values what your employees have to say.

Argument 7 I can't let my employees share in decision making because if I accept their recommendation and it turns out badly, I'll be held responsible for it.

My Response It is true that you will be held responsible for any bad decision made, whether it be your own or that of your subordinates. But why should this cause any special difficulties? You simply don't accept poor decisions, whether they be yours or your subordinates.

When you add up all the arguments and counter-arguments, one simple conclusion stands clear: Managers have much more to gain than lose by involving their subordinates in the decision-making process. Workers like to feel they have a say in their destiny, that they are "in on things" and can claim some ownership of the policies that affect their lives. That's the way employees are, and refusing to accept them as they are isn't going to change them—it will simply frustrate and demotivate them. When it comes to giving out rewards in the workplace, don't forget the value of involving your employees in the decision-making process.

Reward 8: Leisure Time

Item A worker in Wisconsin decides to share his job with another employee. His pay is cut in half, but he explains, "I want more time to fool around with my tenor sax."

Item A certified public accountant limits her practice so that she has time to write the great American novel.

Item A husband and wife both cut their working hours so that they can spend more time at home with their family.

Item A successful salesman takes a whopping cut in commissions so that he can have ample opportunity to fish and hunt.

The salesman, the husband and wife, the accountant, the Wisconsin employee—all have one thing in common: they want to cut their working hours so that they'll have more time to do other things. And they're willing to take a corresponding cut in pay to get their wish. "People say time is money; well, I say less money is more time," is the way one worker explained it.

Such attitudes should come as no surprise. As I indicated earlier, as workers have found their basic needs satisfied, they have developed other, higher level needs—and the need for *leisure time* is one such need.

There are several ways that you as a manager can take advantage of this need for leisure time and use it to create greater worker satisfaction and productivity on the job. It involves using leisure time as a reward. Let me give you two examples of how this can be done

Tactic 1: Leisure Time Tied to Production Rate With this tactic, employees are free to leave the workplace once they have produced a specified number of products or completed a defined amount of work. As an example, let's assume you manage a group of employees who produce wickets for the international market. Let us assume further that ten wickets is the daily acceptable production output per worker. Using the leisure-time-tied-to-production-rate tactic, you allow employees to leave the workplace once they have produced their ten wickets. Thus an employee who has worked diligently can leave early and gain more leisure time. Of course, the quality of wicket production has to remain satisfactory—and to make sure it does, you will probably want to institute a quality control check to maintain standards.

Tactic 2: Redistribution of Working Hours This tactic allows you to give workers more leisure time by rearranging work hours rather than reducing time.[9] You determine an acceptable number of hours per week a worker should be on the job; then you let the individual employees determine when each will put in those hours. Of course, this tactic can only be utilized in situations where hours can be shifted without a deleterious effect on the business.

Here is an example of how Tactic 2 might be utilized in the workplace. Let us assume you are a manager in a company where the following conditions exist: (1) your subordinates currently work a 40-hour week: 8 hours a day, 5 days a week; (2) their work is the kind that can be conducted in a 4-day workweek without any loss in profits; and (3) it is also the kind of work that can be done, without additional personal risk or loss in quality, for 10 hours a day. If these three conditions exist, you meet with your subordinates and give them the choice of working four 10-hour days or five 8-hour days per week. If your workers favor the 4-day week and the accompanying 3-day weekend, then you have just established a ++ relationship. Your employees get a redistribution of working hours they find more to their liking (employee goal); and you still get 40 hours of work from your

---

9. Technically, you are not really giving workers more leisure time by rearranging work hours, but *psychologically* it seems that way to the worker, and that's what counts.

subordinates (management goal). Everybody wins, nobody loses. And that's what good management is all about.

This redistribution-of-time tactic can also be used to set starting and stopping hours for daily work. For instance, some employees might hate coming to work at 8 A.M. but would be very glad to stay at work until 7 P.M. Why not let them come in at 10 A.M. and work until 7 P.M. Again, assuming their work won't be affected by the different hours, this might be a viable way to satisfy a worker's special time needs and still get the required number of work hours.

In today's energy-conscious world, the redistribution of time is becoming increasingly popular. Already the rigid, fixed-hour work-week is giving way to more flexible time spans based on individual company and employee requirements. This new development is called "flextime" in the literature, and don't be surprised if you see a lot more of it in the years to come. This is as it should be. As one politician wisely observed: "The standard 40-hour workweek has been a sacred cow since the depression. Well, we have different problems now." One of those problems is the present-day worker who has a need for more leisure time. When you use time as a reward, you'll be able to satisfy that need and get more productive employees in the bargain.

Reward 9: Feedback

I'd like you to stop for a moment, close your eyes, and try to re-create in your memory several recent cartoons you have seen that deal with business people. Try to re-create as much of each cartoon as you can remember. Now—did you notice any similarities among the cartoons? Any common elements? Let me suggest one: the business chart. In almost every business cartoon I've seen, particularly those featuring a business manager, there is a performance chart in the scene. It may be on the back wall of the office, on a desk, or maybe on an easel or blackboard—but somewhere there is a business performance chart, jagged lines and all.

It's no accident that the business manager and the business chart have been linked in the cartoonist's art and the public's eye. To business managers, *knowledge of how they are doing* is very important—and the business chart is one way that knowledge is recorded and displayed.

This brings us to the topic of *feedback*. Feedback is knowledge of results—information that lets us know how well we're doing at a specific task. Here's an example. Imagine you are visiting your first English pub and your host challenges you to a game of darts. Never having played, you graciously decline and then—in the finest American spirit—run out, buy a set, and begin practicing in your hotel. After the first hundred tosses you begin getting a feel for the game; by the next day, you're ready to go out and challenge the Queen's finest.

You have learned your dart game well. But let us pretend you were forced to practice your throws blindfolded and with plugs in your ears. Could you ever perfect your toss under these conditions? No. Improvement would be impossible because you lacked the vital component of learning: feedback concerning your performance. Deprived of visual feedback—unable to gain knowledge of the results of your dart throwing—your plight would be hopeless.

We use feedback so regularly in our everyday life that we seldom realize how pervasive and important it is. It is only when we are suddenly deprived of our normal opportunity to receive feedback—for instance, in the case of sudden blindness—that we come to understand it momentous value for our very survival.

Because feedback is essential for improving performance, one would think it would be used extensively in the business world. Sadly, most managers don't even come close to providing their employees with adequate knowledge of results to maximize effective performance. And what makes this doubly tragic is that feedback, for many employees, is more than simply a way to improve performance, it is also a *reward* that can satisfy personal needs and lead to greater satisfaction and productivity in the workplace. In other words, workers need feedback to improve their performance, and they want feedback to know how they're doing. The need to know is deeply ingrained in the human character, and particularly in the character of the business manager. Managers have their business performance charts on the wall—why shouldn't subordinates have feedback, too?

In a very informative article, Professor Robert Kreitner identifies three different kinds of feedback you can give your employees to help bolster their satisfaction and productivity in the workplace.

Types of Feedback

1 Informational Feedback This type of feedback helps employees find out how well they are performing on the job. For example, a professor might be handed her course evaluation results or a telephone solicitor could be given information on how many of his contacts actually purchased a particular product. Such knowledge of results should help the professor and solicitor improve job performance in the future. Informational feedback is *nonevaluative*—in other words, it should be transmitted to the employee without judgment as to how good or bad the performance was.

2 Corrective Feedback A manager can be evaluative (judgmental) in providing an employee with knowledge of results. The purpose of corrective feedback, however, is not to criticize and punish but, rather, to inform and correct. The famous basketball coach John Wooden, of the University of California, Los Angeles, was a master at using corrective feedback effectively:

> Observation of Wooden's behavior in practice sessions showed that while 50% of his contacts with his players amounted to straightforward instructions, no less than 75% of his contacts were instructive in nature. He used instructions to simultaneously point out a mistake and indicate the correct way of performing. Wooden's corrective feedback centered around the task at hand, not around the personality of the player. . . An effective manager, like an effective coach, must not only point out mistakes but also get the individual headed in the right direction with appropriate instructions.[10]

3 Reinforcing Feedback When an employee is successful (productive) in the workplace reinforcing feedback is used to reward the job performance. The praise given to employees at Emery Air Freight Corporation (see Chapter 6) is an example of reinforcing feedback (simply telling them how they did would be an example of informational feedback). Which kind of reinforcing feedback you give your workers will depend on their particular needs. As Kreitner correctly observes:

> Managers can . . . diagnose the specific reinforcing consequences to which subordinates currently respond. Careful observation of job performance soon reveals whether or not an individual responds to praise, money, additional responsibility, job rotation, status symbols, formal recognition, peer approval, or any other of the many consequences of job behavior. In a manner of speaking, managers must "fine-tune" reinforcing feedback to suit the individual. No quick and easy panaceas exist in this area.[11].

10. R. Kreitner, "People Are Systems, Too: Filling the Feedback Vacuum," *Business Horizons,* November 1977, pp. 56–57.
11. Ibid., p. 57.

Providing Feedback

There are many opportunities for you to provide employees with feedback on the job. It can be done during formalized time periods set aside for it (for instance, during performance appraisals) or spontaneously during the workday in response to particular employee behavior. To be most effective, feedback should be *specific* and *clearly understandable* to the worker. Feedback won't help if your employees can't identify it with the behavior you're talking about; likewise, telling subordinates how they have performed in statistical terms won't make a difference if they don't understand statistics in the first place.

Don't forget that feedback is essential to learning—and it can be rewarding, too. When you manage, why not make it a part of your worthplace; if you do, you'll increase the chances that your business charts will be looking up.

Reward 10: Social Participation

Do you recall Mr. Monotone, the professor who liked to scratch his head? We got him to increase his little habit by giving him social approval—a reward that satisfied his social needs.

Many workers—managers as well as their subordinates—respond with greater productivity and satisfaction when their social needs are fulfilled in the workplace. This is because many of us are concerned with *affiliation*: being around other people and being accepted by them. People with social needs want to "belong"; they desire social relationships and the chance to interact with others—desires that can be satisfied in the worthplace if a manager provides the proper environment for social participation to take place.

Basically, there are two types of social participation that can be rewarding for a worker on the job: interaction with peers and interaction with the manager.

Types of Social Participation

1 Interaction with Peers We have already seen (in our discussion of job enrichment) how autonomous work teams are created to help fend off boredom and make the working experience more rewarding. In your own managerial situation there will normally be ample opportunity to encourage the development of compatible work groups as a means of satisfying social needs through social participation. One way to do this is participative management (see Reward 7), having subordinates meet as a group with the supervisor to discuss various issues that affect them. Another way is the development of "company spirit" (see Reward 11), encouraging social participation through various social events and team-building efforts.

2 Interaction with the Manager This is an area many supervisors overlook, sometimes with serious consequences. It is important to realize that in many cases the social relationships you establish with your subordinates can have a definite impact on their productivity level and job satisfaction. Managers who are also *leaders* develop effective interpersonal relationships with employees—they are able to transmit a sense of caring and interpersonal enthusiasm which workers appreciate (see chapter 9).

Of course, there are times when interpersonal interaction won't be a vital factor in the workplace. First of all, not all workers have social needs, and if they don't, then the reward value of social participation will be diminished. Secondly, not all jobs allow for social participation. How, for example, can a manager who oversees a group of salespeople working separate territories encourage social participation on the job? Finally, on some jobs the employees might prefer to work alone or, when placed together, become too competitive or hostile with each other.

As with all the rewards in this chapter, you as manager will have to test social participation to see if it's effective in your particular work environment. Does social participation make your subordinates more productive and satisfied? If it does, then fine—it can be used with good results. If it doesn't, well—there are thirteen other rewards waiting to be used. Chances are excellent that some of them will help you get the results you're looking for.

Reward 11: Company Spirit

In central Florida there is a company that makes small aircraft, the kind that hold four to six passengers. It is not a large-scale operation—but it is a spirited one. Each time a plane rolls off the assembly line, the employees are given time off to gather around the finished aircraft and have a celebration (sometimes a picnic), a kind of "product send-off party" when the new owner comes to take delivery of his plane.

Across the country, a California-based Corporation gives its employees "inspirational" gifts—everything from frisbees to T-shirts—in an attempt to "motivate the work force" and "make people aware that their small unit is part of a large company."

What do these two companies have in common? Both organizations are directly fostering esprit de corps among company employees—attempting to increase worker production and satisfaction through the development of company spirit.

Exactly what is company spirit? Company spirit is a sense of pride, dedication, and loyalty to the organization one works for. It's kind of like patriotism, but in this case employees feel a sense of commitment to their employer. When workers feel this way about the company they work for—when they have company spirit—chances are they will be highly productive and satisfied on the job.

By now you are probably asking "How can I, as a manager, create a sense of esprit de corps among my employees?" You might want to try one or more of the suggestions below. Each has been used successfully in the business community. Whether any or all of these approaches work for you will depend, to a great degree, on the size of your work force, the needs of your particular employees, your budget, and the willingness of your organization to actively support "company spirit" programs in the workplace.

1. Develop work teams throughout the company or among the employees you supervise (see Reward 10).
2. Involve employees in the decision-making activities of the company (see Reward 7).
3. Sponsor various social functions for company employees (for example, picnics and outings).
4. Sponsor company sports teams.
5. Undertake activities that will make your employees proud to be associated with the company. For example, some businesses sponsor little league teams or civic activities; others conduct advertising campaigns that emphasize the "good deeds" they are doing in the community.
6. Conduct friendly competitions between various work teams in the company (for example, give an award to the team with highest output or best safety record). Be careful, however, to make sure the competition doesn't get out of hand.

7. Help your employees identify with the products they produce. Some businesses, like the aircraft company in the earlier example, do this by inviting all employees to see the product once it's completed. Other organizations encourage employee identification by having them sign the product they produce or in a like manner have them take personal responsibility for what they have created.

In many ways, a caring organization—one that practices the human use of human resources—will almost automatically increase its chances of developing company spirit. A caring company is like a caring manager—it brings out the best in workers, including higher productivity and job satisfaction.

Reward 12: The Opportunity to Achieve and Advance in the Organization

When employees reach the upper rungs of the Maslow hierarchy, they become responsive to rewards that satisfy their esteem and self-actualization needs. The opportunity to achieve is important to these individuals; so is the opportunity to advance—to be promoted, to rise in the organization.

Time and time again I have watched businesses lose their most capable employees because they failed to provide them with jobs where accomplishment and advancement were possible. Don't make such a mistake. Keep apprised of your employees' progress and check with them frequently to see how they feel about their development within the company.

Do your best to see that all employees have job assignments where achievement and advancement are possible. Many times this will require changing your workers' assignments and responsibilities to keep pace with their growth and development in the workplace (see the discussion of job enrichment under Reward 6). This will require some effort, but it will be effort well invested—particularly when you consider that the people who want to achieve and advance in the organization are normally the most motivated and capable employees you'll be supervising. You don't want to lose them, and making it possible for them to achieve and advance in the organization is one good way to keep them productive, satisfied—and around.

Reward 13: Degrees of Freedom at Work

I recently spoke with a department store buyer who was angry because she might have to punch in and out of work on a time clock. "I didn't have to do that under the old manager," she argued.

"What about the other people in your office," I inquired, "don't they have to punch in and out?"

"They're hourly workers," the buyer scoffed, "I'm a professional, I don't work by the clock."

Although this particular employee sounds a bit egotistical and spoiled, her concern does reflect a problem common to many workers as they climb the organizational ladder and the Maslow hierarchy: the need for more degrees of freedom on the job.

When I speak of degrees of freedom in work, I am referring to the level of personal autonomy and responsibility a person has on the job. Employees with high degrees of freedom in the workplace are pretty much their own boss when it comes to organizing their work and making decisions. Employees with low degrees of freedom have very little say in what they do or how they do it—they are, as some managers are fond of saying, "closely watched."

Now it is true that some types of jobs require closer supervision than others. It is also true that certain workers prefer to be closely supervised and shun the opportunity for more personal autonomy in the workplace. In these cases, giving workers degrees of freedom can cause difficulties. But what about those jobs that *can* be effectively performed by employees working under their own "recognizance"? And what about those workers who covet more degrees of freedom in the workplace? In these circumstances managers would be well-advised to loosen the reins of control and let employees have more say in the conduct of their work.

To determine what level of freedom you should give your workers, ask (and answer) these two questions:

1. Are my employees doing the kind of work that requires constant managerial supervision, or can I step back and let them have more control over their job activities?
2. Do my employees want more degrees of freedom on the job?

As far as the second question is concerned, you won't go very far afield if you follow this guideline. Generally, employees with higher level needs will be most rewarded by greater degrees of freedom on the job. If you turn back to Figure 5.2 you will note three things self-actualizing people want out of a job: (1) creative and challenging work; (2) responsibility for decision making; and (3) flexibility and freedom. These three wants can be satisfied by giving your employees greater degrees of freedom in the workplace. And if they're capable workers, giving them greater freedom will make your job easier in the bargain!

Reward 14: Pleasant Forms of Moderate Distraction

Way back in 1965 a team of behavioral scientists conducted an interesting study with some Yale University undergraduates. One group of students read a series of four persuasive messages in a room well stocked with soft drinks and peanuts. The students were encouraged to sample the refreshments as they read—which they all did. A second group of students was presented with the same four messages to read, but in a room where no refreshments were available. Both groups of students were asked, before and after reading the four messages, certain key questions, which enabled the investigators to assess their degree of opinion change (if any) in response to the persuasive appeals. In other words, the scientists were able to ascertain if any of the students had been swayed by the four persuasive appeals.

What were the results of the study? The students who ate while they read were more persuaded by each of the four messages than were those students who read the same messages without food.[12]

On the basis of this study and several others,[13] behavioral scientists now believe that, in general, *persuasive appeals become more powerful when presented in conjunction with moderately distracting stimuli (for example, food) which positively reward the individual.*

---

12. I. Janis, D. Kaye, and P. Kirschner, "Facilitating Effects of 'Eating-While-Reading' on Responsiveness to Persuasive Communications," *Journal of Personality and Social Psychology*, vol. 1, 1965, pp. 181–186.

13. See M. Karlins and H. Abelson, *Persuasion: How Opinions and Attitudes Are Changed*, Springer, New York, 1970

How can this information be of use to you as a manager on the job? it suggests that if you want to be more persuasive with your employees (have them do what you want them to do), it might help if you utilize some pleasant forms of moderate distraction while making your requests. Even more important, pleasant forms of moderate distraction can increase worker satisfaction, not only because they are rewards in themselves, but also because they act as a boredom reducer in the workplace (see *Job Enrichment* under Reward 6).

There are several kinds of pleasant distraction you can use in the workplace (such as music and workspace alterations), but the most practical, versatile, and effective one for our purposes is ...*food*.

Salespeople have long recognized and utilized the power of food. The selling power of the client lunch is widely accepted in business circles. When it comes time to sign the contract—to close the deal—it is often accomplished over dessert. "A well-fed customer is a purchasing customer," as one salesperson expressed it.

Does this mean you'll have to take your subordinates to dinner every time you want to use pleasant forms of moderate distraction? Definitely not. The bent-elbow-and-heaping-forkful approach might be suitable for special occasions, but it is certainly inappropriate as an everyday kind of reward at work. It is appropriate, however, to serve coffee and doughnuts at staff meetings—particularly if the meetings are early in the morning. Even if you have to pay for these "goodies" out of pocket, I think you will find the benefits far outweigh the costs. It is amazing how a few doughnuts and cups of coffee can perk people up and put them in a cooperative, productive frame of mind. I know managers who also have coffee and small bowls of snacks in their offices, to offer to subordinates when they come in to discuss items of business. According to the managers, this helps open channels of communication and creates good feelings.

Like all the rewards we have discussed in this chapter, pleasant forms of moderate distraction will work better in some job settings than others. How effective will the reward be with your employees? The best way to find out is give pleasant distractions a try in your workplace.

Some Recommendations

1 Use Moderate, Not Intense, Distractions If a distraction is too strong, it can cause a decrease (rather than an increase) in productivity. For example, some companies pipe music over their intercoms. If this music is too distracting, employees end up concentrating on the tunes rather than on their work.

2 Use Pleasant, Not Unpleasant, Distractions Research studies clearly show that unpleasant distractions (even moderate forms of unpleasant distractions) reduce worker satisfaction and productivity—exactly the opposite of what you want. In this context, be sure you *know* what your individual employees consider pleasant or unpleasant distractions. For example, some employees might find hard rock music a pleasant form of moderate distraction, while others might consider it an unpleasant form of intense distraction. Play it safe: observe your workers' reactions to the distractions you use. That way you'll know what they think about them.

Work as Its Own Reward

In this chapter I have described fourteen rewards you can use to make your employees more productive and satisfied in the workplace.

"But," you ask, "what if my employees are already satisfied with their work?" In that case, count yourself among the fortunate. As management expert Lewis Moore indicates: "The more rewarding the work is perceived to be by the worker, the less the need for supervision—except to specify results wanted."[14]

Unfortunately, not that many workers are naturally turned on by their jobs, and "in order to get the same level of motivation from employees who perceive less reward in their work, the difference in reinforcement must come from management. . . ."[15]

This is where you come in. If your workers are not already satisfied with their jobs, you can help them by utilizing the fourteen rewards to create an environment that fulfills their needs and turns the workplace into a worthplace. In other words, your goal is to use rewards to create a worthplace more satisfying and meaningful to each individual employee.

Work does not have to be a four-letter word. Through such techniques as job enrichment, social participation, and employee involvement in decision making, you can encourage employees to get "into" what they are doing—help build a job to a point where it will become intrinsically interesting and motivationally self-sustaining.

Of course, you won't always be successful in getting an employee to the point where work becomes its own reward; but even then you can use rewards like praise, public recognition, and leisure time to make the job more palatable. Either way, you accomplish your ultimate goal: making the workplace a worthplace, where employees can satisfy their needs and be more productive at the same time.

14. Cited in M. Karlins "To the Manager Who Wants to Lead," Paper presented at the National Convention of AHRMOB, New Orleans, Louisiana, November 19, 1986, p. 3.
15. Ibid.

How to Administer Workplace Rewards Most Effectively

8

Knowing the rewards you can use on the job is important, but you must also learn the rules for using those rewards most effectively.

Aerospace industry manager

Before I present the rules for administering workplace rewards most effectively, let me briefly re-state the major points discussed earlier.

A Brief Review

From our discussion of behavior modification and Maslow's need hierarchy you now know that (1) individual workers have individual needs and will behave in ways that lead to the satisfaction of those needs and that (2) behavior which is rewarded will be maintained or even increase in frequen-cy. Putting this information together, your goal as a manager is to reinforce appropriate work be-havior with rewards that satisfy the particular needs of individual employees. This should enhance worker productivity and satisfy worker needs, thus establishing the ++ relationship essential to making the workplace a worthplace.

Accomplishing this goal will require you to complete successfully a three-step process:

Step 1 You will have to identify the specific needs of your individual workers.

Step 2 You will have to satisfy each worker's specific need(s) with the appropriate reward(s)

Step 3 You will have to administer worker rewards effectively.

Step 1 is discussed in Chapter 5 and at the end of Chapter 6. Step 2 is discussed in Chapter 7, where you will find the fourteen rewards you can use in motivating your workers. Step 3 is dis-cussed below. Here you will find the basic guidelines for administering rewards in a manner that maximizes worker productivity and satisfaction on the job.

Some Major Guidelines for Administering Rewards Effectively

Guideline 1 Know what kind of performance you want from your employees and let them know what your expectations are.

To administer rewards effectively, both you and your employees should have a common un-derstanding of what is considered effective behavior (good output) on the job. This means you should first determine in your own mind the kinds of employee action that will lead to good job per-formance, and then you should explain to your subordinates what steps they can take to achieve that good performance and receive rewards.

If you don't take the time to tell your employees what your performance goals are and how they can be reached, then your subordinates will have to find out for themselves, usually through trial-and-error behavior on the job—and that is a tremendous waste of time, effort, and productivity. It doesn't do much for creating job satisfaction either.

Here are three questions I'd like you to ask yourself as a manager:

1. Have I determined what constitutes good performance in the workplace?
2. Have I communicated to my employees (a) my definition and standard of good performance; (b) the kinds of job behavior they should undertake to achieve good job performance; and (c) what they must do to receive the various rewards?
3. Do I have a method of accurately and fairly assessing the level of worker performance on the job?

If you can answer yes to all three questions, then you're in good shape as far as Guideline 1 is concerned.

Guideline 2 Give your subordinates those rewards that best satisfy their particular needs.

Put another way, the reward that works best is the reward that satisfies a worker's need(s) most successfully. Your goal should be the achievement of a match between workers' needs and the rewards they receive on the job. To do this effectively, you should know about the kinds of needs employees have and the rewards associated with them.

Some managers try to guess what needs their workers have and what rewards they'd like to receive. As we saw in Chapter Five this can lead to some very inaccurate estimates. If you want to obtain greatest accuracy in identifying which rewards work best with which employees, observe your subordinates as you give them reinforcement. That way you can pinpoint the rewards that work best with each employee. Such information is particularly valuable, because in most instances you'll have to pick from a number of different rewards to use at any given need level of the Maslow hierarchy.

Also, continue to observe your subordinates even *after* you have ascertained their needs and the rewards they value most. This is crucial because workers' needs can change over time, and so can their attitudes toward particular rewards. For example, some workers get bored with certain rewards if they're used too often, causing them to lose their effectiveness. If you continue to observe your subordinates, you will be alerted to these changes and be able to take corrective action. Otherwise, you might miss such changes entirely and wonder why you suddenly wind up with a disgruntled, unproductive employee.

Remember, the best way to see if a reward "works" is to administer it to an employee and watch the results. If the rewarded behavior is maintained or increases in frequency, chances are the reward is effective.

In observing Guideline 2, it will help to keep the following points in mind (in addition to those already mentioned):

1. Many employees have several different needs at the same time, thus allowing you to use several different kinds of rewards in such circumstances.
2. Certain rewards (such as money) can satisfy more than one human need, and certain needs can be satisfied by more than one reward. Choose the reward that works best for the individual worker in question.

3. Be on the lookout for boredom effects if you use the same reward frequently with a particular employee. Try not to overuse a reinforcement so that it loses its effectiveness. Using more than one kind of reward, or decreasing use of the same reward, will reduce the risk of "reward boredom."

4. Try to familiarize yourself with all fourteen rewards and how they can be used to best advantage. The more rewards you can utilize comfortably and effectively, the better manager you'll be.

Guideline 3 You don't have to reward a desired behavior everytime it occurs.

Many managers believe that the best way to keep employee performance high is to reinforce effective behavior everytime it occurs. In reality, quite the opposite can occur: rewarding specific actions everytime they occur can actually decrease performance levels in the long run.

Initially, when an employee is learning a new task, it helps to reward the employee frequently, so that the behavior becomes fixed in the person's response pattern. Once the behavior has become established, however, it is appropriate to *gradually* cut back the frequency of rewards and move toward *intermittent* ("variable") reinforcement of effective performance. By rewarding behavior intermittently (rather than everytime it occurs) you gain three benefits:

1. You don't need as much of the reward (for instance, if you're using money as a reinforcement, it will last longer if administered intermittently rather than continuously).

2. The chance that the worker becomes bored with the reward through overuse will be reduced.

3. Intermittent reinforcement sustains higher levels of performance over longer periods of time. Employees keep working with the expectation that their reward is "right around the corner." This type of thinking keeps gamblers frantically pumping coins into slot machines.

Now comes an interesting question. How intermittent should your intermittent reinforcement be? In other words, how often should you reward your employees for work well done? The answer is, often enough to sustain quality job performance. When you use reinforcement, observe the impact of your rewards on your employees' behavior. If worker performance level remains high, chances are that your frequency of reinforcement is "on target." If performance drops, however, you might want to decrease or increase the amount of reinforcement until you reach a level that brings employee performance up to optimum levels. In doing so, the following points might help:

1. Too much as well as too little reinforcement can lead to a decline in job performance. Do not reinforce so frequently that the reward loses potency or so infrequently as to "extinguish" appropriate behaviors.

2. Different employees require different amounts of reinforcement to keep their performance levels high. By observing your workers, you will be able to determine the ideal intermittent schedule for any particular employee.

Guideline 4 Reward desired behaviors immediately after they occur.

The sooner you can reward an employee for superior job performance, the more effective that reinforcement will be. Conversely, the longer the delay between the desired behavior and the ensuing reward, the less effective the reinforcement becomes. This timing-of-reinforcement effect is clearly documented in the behavioral science literature and says, in effect, that you must act quickly once you become aware of reinforceable behavior.

75

Of course, sometimes it is not possible for a manager to reinforce an employee immediately for desired work behavior. For example, two weeks may pass before a manager learns that a salesperson has closed a big deal; or a manager may be away from the office when an employee does something outstanding. What then? Fortunately, reinforcement is still possible, but under these circumstances it is vitally important that the manager clearly state what the reward is for. It is not enough to say, "This bonus is for good work on the job." The work behavior in question must be specifically identified by saying, for example, "This bonus is to recognize your achievement in closing the Johnson account." It is necessary that the worker establish a bond between a specific reward and a specific behavior—otherwise behavior modification won't work. And it's up to you as manager to reinforce in a manner that makes such bonding possible.

Guideline 5 Whenever possible use reward rather than punishment in the workplace.

Perhaps you've wondered why I spent a whole chapter discussing workplace rewards and not a single page examining punishments. It is because I believe that rewards are more effective in establishing desired behaviors and avoiding undesirable ones. Even when punishment does "work" in controlling behavior there can be significant "downside" risks in using such an approach:

1. an employee who is punished into compliance doesn't usually perform to the best of his/her ability . . . rather, he/she does just enough to get by and avoid further management sanctions;

2. an employee who is punished into compliance will often return to his/her undesirable behavior(s) once the manager is not around;

3. in extreme circumstances, punished employees have been known to commit acts of violence against the manager and/or acts of sabotage against company equipment/products.

Much of my thinking about reward versus punishment is reflected in the fable of the old man and his coat. It seems the old gent was spotted by the spirits of Winter and Summer as he walked along a path in an enchanted forest. The two spirits were in a competitive mood that afternoon, and suddenly the spirit of Winter said, "I'll bet you I can strip that man of the coat he's wearing faster than you can." "It's a bet," the spirit of summer replied, "you can go first."

The spirit of Winter took a deep breath and blew up a raging arctic storm that whipped through the forest and buffeted the old man about like a leaf. He gathered his tattered coat around him and hung on for dear life. The wind threatened to tear the coat right off his body. Every button was ripped away, and still the old man hung on gamely. Finally, the spirit of Winter tired and the storm dissipated. The old man brushed the debris off what was left of his coat and took a few tentative steps.

"It's my turn now," said the spirit of Summer, and with a nod sent the clouds scurrying across the sky and turned the sun's full radiance on the forest. The old man turned his face to the sun and felt the welcome, penetrating heat. It felt good. He took off his coat and continued on his way.

The moral? it is better if an employee wants to do something than if he has to do it. This is the spirit and essence of the human use of human resources; the cornerstone of the ++ relationship in the worthplace.

Does this mean I'm against all punishment in the workplace? No. There will be times when, having exhausted all avenues of positive reinforcement, your only recourse will be punitive action. Yet, even then, punishment can be administered in a constructive fashion—not for revenge but to get the worker back "on track." And, of course, punishment should always be done in private, as your goal is to educate, not humiliate, an employee.

Administered in the proper spirit—as a form of constructive criticism—even punishment can play a meaningful role in the worthplace. Before you opt for using it, however, it might be instructive to consider the words of management authority Bernard Rosenbaum: "When it comes to supervising people, rarely is there too much positive reinforcement. Managers who encounter undesirable behavior should ask themselves when and in what way the desired behavior was last reinforced."

Guideline 6 Give rewards only when they are deserved.

In other words, reinforcement should be sincere and earned. If an employee doesn't deserve praise, then don't give it; it is better to withhold a compliment than give one dishonestly. Not only is such behavior unethical, it is bad management. Employees are quick to detect your motives; they see such reinforcement as cheap manipulation—which it is. Don't behave in such a manner; it is not humane and it doesn't work.

A Personal View of Effective Leadership

9

The lack of leadership in industry and government is the chief difficulty in this country.

William McCleery

I love to browse through bookstores. On a recent visit I noticed that an entire shelf was set aside for books on sexual techniques. Above the shelf someone had written a note claiming, "These techniques can make *you* a better lover." While I was mulling over that bit of advertising, a student walked up and showed me an armload of business books she had just purchased. "I want to make it big in my job," she explained, "and these books have the techniques I'll need to know to become an effective leader."

Do you find all this lamentable? I do. It is a sad commentary on the human condition that people believe effective loving or leading can be reduced to a series of techniques.

Please don't misunderstand me. I'm not saying that techniques are unimportant—they just aren't the whole story or, for that matter, the most important part of it. Take leadership, for example. There are literally dozens of techniques you can use to become a more effective supervisor, but those techniques by themselves won't make you a true leader. There is an ingredient missing, something else that has to be there. It's like trying to bake bread without yeast. You can still do it, but you'll never get the dough to rise past a certain point. As a manager you can use the various techniques to sharpen your supervisory skills, but you'll never *rise* to great leadership without adding the missing ingredient—the ingredient I call the "human component" of leadership.

What, exactly, is this human component so crucial for effective leadership? It is actually three things: *love, enthusiasm, and dedication.* It is no wonder that the first letters of these four words add up to another word:

L OVE + E NTHUSIASM + A ND + D EDICATION = L.E.A.D.

The manager who knows how to L.E.A.D. becomes a L.E.A.D.E.R., because L OVE, E NTHUSIASM, A ND D EDICATION E ARN R ESPECT—and that is basic to a meaningful bond between manager and employee.[1]

Love, Enthusiasm, and Dedication Defined

These words have special meanings when utilized in the workplace, so it is best that we define them now.

---

1. Cited in M. Karlins & E. Hargis, "Beyond Leadership: The Human Factor in Leadership," *Management Solutions,* August, 1988, 18–21.

Love Another word for this term is "caring." What I am referring to here is the capacity of managers to love (in a caring sense) their employees, to sincerely care for them as human beings. This sense of caring is something which can be learned but can't be faked. Workers are quick to sense whether their managers truly care for them. If employees feel this caring is present, it can contribute mightily to their productivity and satisfaction in the workplace. If, on the other hand, they feel a manager lacks this capacity, then no amount of techniques—however well executed—will ever make that manager a great leader.

Let me illustrate the importance of love/caring with an example from where I work. In my department I have a colleague who is an outstanding scholar and a dedicated academician. I took it for granted he was also a topnotch teacher: after all, he knows his subject matter better than anyone else at the university, and I have seen him spend many hours preparing his lectures. You can imagine my surprise, then, when several students stopped by my office to complain about my colleague's poor teaching performance.

"What's wrong with him," I wanted to know, "Is he a boring speaker?"

"No," they responded.

"Is he unprepared for class?"

"No," again.

"Are his tests unfair?"

"No," again.

"Does he miss classes?"

"No," a fourth time.

"Well, what *is* it then?"

Silence. Finally a student came up with this response: "I guess it's not really his teaching that's the problem . . . it's a feeling I get that he doesn't really *care* about me as a person, that I'm somebody to be tolerated as part of the job."

"That's right," another student broke in. "The man is aloof and distant . . . he doesn't treat his students like human beings."

Love. It's a vital part of effective leadership.

Enthusiasm Enthusiastic managers are persons who put energy into their work, who bring a sense of spirit and excitement to the workplace. Enthusiasm is contagious. If managers have it, chances are better that their workers will have it, too. Lethargy, unfortunately, is also contagious. When managers walk into the office looking disinterested and bored, is it any wonder their employees become listless and unmotivated as well? As a manager you set a mood tone for your employees, and it is important that the mood be s positive one. But, in being enthusiastic, two points are worth remembering:

1. To be enthusiastic you don't have to be "rah rah" or "gung ho." A quiet enthusiasm is just as potent as animated enthusiasm—just so long as employees can sense your positive, interested attitude toward work.

2. As a manager you don't have to be enthusiastic about your work every moment of every working day. Nobody expects you to like your job all the time! There will be days when you come to work in a sour mood; there will also be times when your work gets you down. In these circumstances, it is perfectly all right to act "down in the dumps." Employees don't expect you to feign enthusiasm when you feel like hell. In fact, if you are usually enthusiastic in the workplace, a few "off" days will tend to reinforce that general enthusiasm.

Enthusiasm. It's an important part of the charisma generated by effective leaders.

Dedication Another word for dedication can be "commitment." Dedicated managers are committed to their work, and they pass along this sense of dedication to their employees.

Many managers ask me how they can be sure they're dedicated to their work. This is not a silly question, as being immersed in a job day after day sometimes limits our ability to judge work effectively. There are two ways you can take a reading of your job dedication level.

1. *Monitor your enthusiasm:* Keep tabs on your level of job enthusiasm over time. Dedication and enthusiasm are intimately linked: people who are dedicated to their jobs are almost always enthusiastic about them. Thus if you sense your enthusiasm for work is waning, it might be a sign of eroding dedication as well.

2. *Ask yourself two questions upon awakening in the morning:* (1) Am I looking forward to today? (2) Would I rather be doing something else than the work I'm in? If you find yourself *consistently* answering no to the first question and yes to the second question, it is doubtful you are generating much dedication to your job. And if that's the way *you* feel about your work, how can you expect your employees to feel any differently about theirs?

Dedication. It's a vital source of strength for effective leaders.

A Personal Request

Leadership is more than a series of techniques to be mastered. It is first and foremost a human being *being human.* It is a manager who understands the human component in the leadership equation— who cares about employees and is enthusiastic about and dedicated to the job. It is a manager who uses behavioral science techniques to establish a + + relationship on the job, a *worthplace* where employees can satisfy their needs and be productive at the same time.

Of course, by my definition, there are not many managers who qualify as leaders in the contemporary business world. For that matter there are not many leaders among parents, teachers, and politicians either. That is because most of us have not learned to L.E.A.D. in a humane way.

Which brings me to my request: Just because there are so many inhumane managers in the work world doesn't mean you have to further populate their ranks. *If you feel you cannot or will not inject the human component into your leadership behavior, don't become a manager in the first place—at least not the kind of manager who has to consistently interact with subordinates.* It just won't be fair to you, and it certainly won't be fair to your employees. If your subordinate wants to be uncaring, unenthusiastic, and undedicated on the job, that is bad enough; but if you as a manager feel that way, then you are setting an example that can affect many other lives (as well as your own) in a negative way.

Some of you might not agree with, or honor, this request. That is your choice. As the chapter title suggests, this is my personal view of leadership, and you might not share it. But I do believe it is a correct view, and I, for one, certainly wouldn't want to work under a manager who disagreed with it. Think about it, would you?

SECTION THREE

**You Be the Manager:
Exercises and Cases
to Sharpen Your
Managerial Interest
and Skills**

The ManagemARTS Competitions 10

A. Purpose of these competitions:

1. To stimulate interest in the field of management.

2. To stimulate interest in artistic expression.

3. To encourage the utilization of artistic expression to depict and describe various aspects of management.

4. To accumulate relevant artistic creations for use in management class lectures and books.

B. Competition eligibility:

All students enrolled in this course are eligible to compete in any or all of the ManagemARTS Competitions.

C. The competitions:

There are three separate ManagemARTS Competitions.

1. *ManagemART—Photography Competition:* Any photograph relevant to the topic of management is eligible for submission as long as it is original (taken by the contestant). Entries should be suitably mounted if possible (a piece of tagboard will be fine).

2. *ManagemART—Artwork Competition:* Any piece of art (painting, sculpture, collage, etc.) relevant to the topic of management is eligible for submission as long as it is original (created by the contestant).

3. *ManagemART—Poetry Competition:* Any poem with a theme relevant to the topic of management is eligible for submission as long as it is original (written by the contestant).

D. Criteria for judgment of entries:

Entries will be judged according to three criteria: (1) relevance to management (we define "management" as those topics that appear in your course text(s) and/or class lectures); (2) originality; (3) skill in using your chosen medium. *Remember:* The boundaries of management (as defined in class lectures and texts) and the scope of your own imagination are the only limits to the degree of creativity possible in these competitions. The course instructor will be the official judge of all competition entries . . . and his/her decisions are final.

E. Submission of entries:

All entries should be submitted to the course instructor either at the end of any class or during scheduled office hours. You can submit as many entries in as many competitions as you wish. Each entry must include the official ENTRY FORM, fully filled out and signed by the contestant. Several entry forms can be found in this book. If you do not wish to tear these forms out of the book (or you need more forms than are provided), please make copies of the forms, and use the copies with your entry submissions.

F. Deadline for submission of entries:

All entries must be received by the course instructor no later than one month before the last day of the current academic term.

G. Prizes for winning entries:

Awards for the ManagemART Competitions will be announced early in the term. Such prizes need not be given, however, if, in the course instructor's opinion, submissions are not of a quality level to justify awards.

ManagemARTS Competitions

Entry Form*

Instructions: Please provide all the information requested and be sure to sign your name at the bottom of the page. Thank you.

(Check one): My entry is for. . . .   _____ Photography Competition

                                             _____ Artwork Competition

                                             _____ Poetry Competition

Name: _____

Social Security #: _____

Date: _____

Please read and sign:

By my signature below I hereby certify that the photograph, artwork or poem I am entering in the ManagemART Competition is original (created by myself) and not the work of another person. I also agree to let the course instructor use, at his/her discretion, my entry in his/her classes and/or published works without compensation due me or the need for my permission.

Signed: _____

*Please use a separate entry form for each entry you submit. Thank you.

ManagemARTS Competitions

Entry Form*

Instructions: Please provide all the information requested and be sure to sign your name at the bottom of the page. Thank you.

(Check one): My entry is for. . . .   _____   Photography Competition

                                         _____   Artwork Competition

                                         _____   Poetry Competition

Name: _____

Social Security #: _____

Date: _____

Please read and sign:

By my signature below I hereby certify that the photograph, artwork or poem I am entering in the ManagemART Competition is original (created by myself) and not the work of another person. I also agree to let the course instructor use, at his/her discretion, my entry in his/her classes and/or published works without compensation due me or the need for my permission.

Signed: _____

*Please use a separate entry form for each entry you submit. Thank you.

ManagemARTS Competitions

Entry Form*

Instructions: Please provide all the information requested and be sure to sign your name at the bottom of the page. Thank you.

(Check one): My entry is for. . . .   _____   Photography Competition

_____   Artwork Competition

_____   Poetry Competition

Name: _____

Social Security # _____

Date: _____

Please read and sign:

By my signature below I hereby certify that the photograph, artwork or poem I am entering in the ManagemART Competition is original (created by myself) and not the work of another person. I also agree to let the course instructor use, at his/her discretion, my entry in his/her classes and/or published works without compensation due me or the need for my permission.

Signed: _____

*Please use a separate entry form for each entry you submit. Thank you.

The "Believe It or Not" Management Incidents Hall of Fame

11

A. Purpose of the assignment:

  1. To help the reader understand/appreciate the sometimes unpredictable—and challenging—nature of management

  2. To stimulate reader interest in management . . . and have some fun at the same time.

B. Instructions:

Although some people believe that a manager's job is predictable and even a bit tedious . . . such is often not the case! In fact, managers have been known to get into intriguing predicaments, undergo strange experiences and/or do some pretty zany things.

  To complete this assignment, you are asked to locate a *published* report (in a newspaper, periodical, book, etc) of an *interesting* management incident . . . the kind of incident that makes you want to say ". . . believe it or not . . ." when you describe it to others. This report might chronicle a unique management practice, or possibly recount an incredible managerial experience. Again, what you want to look for is any *published* incident/story that is characterized by a high "interest-grabbing" quotient. If the example is humorous as well as interesting, all the better.

  Once you have located your "believe it or not" management incident please submit it with the completed information form (or copy of the form) which appears on the following page.

  Remember: the more interesting the example submitted, the greater the value it will have. *Interest level* is the only criteria by which each submission will be judged.

The "Believe It or Not" Management
Incidents Hall of Fame

Submission Form

Instructions: Please fill out this form and staple it to the published report (or a copy of that report) of the management incident.

Your Name: _____

Your Soc. Sec. #: _____

Date: _____

Class Starting Time: _____

Author(s) of your published report: _____

_____

Title of the published report: _____

_____

Publication in which report appeared: _____

_____

Page(s) where report appeared: _____

Date of publication: _____

The "Service Ace or Double Fault?" Case Study $\boxed{12}$

Part I: View Two Films
Part II: Group Assignment

Part I: Instructions

In a few minutes you will be seeing two films—*Service Management* and *Remember Me.* At the end of each movie you will be given a brief period of time (5 minutes) to write a synopsis (summary) of the plot which you can refer back to in completing PART II of this exercise.

Service Ace or Double Fault?
Part I

Please write a brief synopsis (summary) of the movie you have just seen, *Service Management.* You will have five (5) minutes to complete this task. Do *not* hand in your summary . . . you will be using it later in the exercise.

Service Ace or Double Fault?
Part I, Continued

Please write a brief synopsis (summary of the movie you have just seen, *Remember Me.* You will have five (5) minutes to complete this task. Do *not* hand in your summary . . . you will be using it later in the exercise.

Service Ace or Double Fault?
Part II

Part II: Instructions

Your group will have 30 minutes to answer the following questions. In answering, be sure to incorporate what you learned from watching *Service Management* and *Remember Me*. Refer back to your summaries in Part 1 if you need to refresh your memory concerning any points made in the films. If you need additional space to answer the questions, please feel free to use extra paper.

The Questions

Do you think that this University practices good customer service, assuming that you, the students, are the customers? If so, give examples of this good service. If not, give examples of poor service and indicate what your group would do to improve customer service. (Please list your answers on the next page.)

Service Ace or Double Fault?
Part II, Continued

Please answer the questions from the previous page in the space below.

After four years of working under John Ashley, Richard Bennett had had it. The work itself was fine – he was in charge of the company's four metal-working plants, knew the work, liked it, and was sure he did a good job. His subordinates were great. Every one of the four plant managers was first-rate, easy to work with, competent, on top of his job. The company was fine and clearly going places. The pay was good.

But Mr. Ashley! Ashley was a pain in every part of Richard's body from top to toe. Never an encouraging word, only grunts of criticism. Richard slaved on the memoranda and reports he sent up to Ashley's office – and he never heard anything about them. He always made sure to be in Ashley's office first thing in the morning with anything important – or to call him at 8:30 sharp. His first boss had drilled that into him when Richard started as a manufacturing engineer. Yet Ashley always acted as if Richard had broken all Ten Commandments when he knocked at the door and asked whether he could come in. "What have you to see me about *again,* Bennett" he'd growl. But he'd also bite his head off if Richard did not tell him to the last detail any single thing that was going on, and especially any bad news ahead. But the worst thing about Ashley was his appalling illiteracy. Richard Bennett – with a B.A. and an M.A. in mechanical engineering from M.I.T. – had then, on his own time, gone and taken all the courses he could get in modern management, in modern production, in operations research and in quantitative methods. Then to have to work for a boss who hadn't even finished high school! Ashley had started as a machinist after his military service. He probably couldn't even do long division and surely could not follow the simplest regression analysis. It was too much!

And so Richard Bennett decided to leave. He realized that he had made the decision on a Sunday evening when he had worked at home on a careful study of order patterns and production schedules, adding up to a recommendation to change production scheduling, inventory control, and shipping schedules for all four plants of the metal-working division. It was the most searching analysis he had yet made, and he felt very good about it. But as he was about to put the pages together for his secretary to type out the following morning he suddenly realized that there was absolutely no point in showing the work to Ashley. "The old coot just couldn't understand," he said to himself. "And if he could, he'd still be much too reactionary to make any changes in what had been procedure since before I was born. He'll never even read the report, I bet. And instead of discussing the figures he'll treat me to one of his endless anecdotes about the good old days. I just can't take any more of it."

And so without even telling his wife, he set about finding another job. He had little difficulty finding one. The new job was not quite as big, not quite as well paid, and with a company that had only limited growth opportunities, but the company was a highly technological one, and so

*"Can You Manage Your Boss," from MANAGEMENT CASES by Peter F. Drucker. Copyright 1977 by Peter F. Drucker. Reprinted by permission of Harper & Row, Publishers, Inc.

Richard's management science knowledge was fully appreciated. Indeed, Richard was now the one who felt somewhat under-educated, since so many of his new associates had Ph.D's. Richard's wife approved of his job move; she had long known how frustrated he had been. Ashley approved in his boorish fashion. When Richard went in to tell him, he only said: "I won't try to talk you out of it. I have to tell you, Bennett, that I could not and would not have recommended you for a promotion. Your leaving makes it much easier for all of us." And so Richard packed his papers and prepared to move out of the office in which he had suffered four long years.

Two days before he left, he had an unexpected visitor, Larry Snyder, the plant manager who was to take Richard's job. Snyder's selection had surprised Richard. He had been sure Ashley would pick the oldest and most conventional of his four plant managers. Instead he chose the youngest—Snyder was well under forty—the most innovative, the boldest. In fact, Richard had to admit to himself that he would have hesitated to take the gamble. Snyder had been plant manager only a few years, and Richard doubted whether he was really ready yet. Richard had gotten along fairly well with Snyder, but did not consider himself close to the man. Richard was therefore somewhat surprised when Snyder called up, said that he was coming to the headquarters building in a day or two and would like a private, off-the-record session at Richards' home. He was even more surprised when Snyder said, "Richard, I was quite shocked when I heard that you were leaving. I was even more shocked when Ashley called me and told me I'd take over from you. I didn't expect a big promotion for another three, four years, if then. What can you tell me that will help me?"

Richard spent an hour or two discussing the plants and their managers, and another hour talking about the relationships and problems inside the company—in particular about a long-standing feud with Purchasing and about the rather prickly personnel department and its failure to back operating management against the union. Finally he said, "Snyder, I guess you know most of this," and Larry Snyder nodded. "But," continued Richard, "the really important thing about this job isn't the plants, it isn't Purchasing or Personnel or the accountants. It is that impossible S. O. B., the boss. He doesn't read a line—you might as well write on water. He never has a word of praise, never, but is quick to criticize. He expects you to keep him informed about everything and is positively indecent in his insistence that you inform him ahead of time of anything unexpected. Yet he bites your head off when you come in to tell him. He is such an old reactionary that you just don't dare propose any change. You'll have no real trouble with any part of your job—it's in good shape, and the men are a pleasure to work with—but you just won't be able to manage the boss."

Richard Bennett soon forgot all about his old company—the new job turned out to be a great deal tougher than he had expected, and kept him fully occupied. He once ran into Ashley at the airport and asked him how Snyder was doing—only to get a gruff "Why should I tell you?" for an answer. So he was quite surprised to read three years later, in the *Wall Street Journal,* that Larry Snyder had been appointed to succeed John Ashley as manufacturing vice-president when Ashley moved up to executive vice-president in charge of the metal-working and mechanical divisions. "I must send Snyder a note of congratulations when I get home tonight," Bennett said to himself. But when he got home he found that Snyder had anticipated him. On the hall table was a huge flower pot with a handwritten note from Snyder:

Dear Richard Bennett,

You will have heard that I have been promoted to VP—Manufacturing—
and I owe it all to you and want to say "Thank you." You have taught me
that I had to learn to manage the boss. And you told me how to do it.

Cordially,
Larry Snyder

"Can You Manage Your Boss" Case Study

Individual Assignment

Instructions: You will have 30 minutes to read the case and answer the following two questions. Please work alone in this phase of the exercise. If you need additional space, please feel free to use extra paper.

Question #1: This case study is designed to help us think and learn about how to manage bosses effectively. In this context, *specify the mistakes you think Richard Bennett made in dealing with the boss (John Ashley).*

1. UNDERESTIMATING THE BOSS'S COMPETENCE/INTELLIGENCE
2. EXPECTED PRAISE
3. DID NOT LEARN ASHLEY'S WAY OF CONDUCTING BUSINESS
4. TOOK CRITICISM THE WRONG WAY
5. DID NOT LEARN TO MANAGE THE BOSS

"Can You Manage Your Boss?" Case Study

"Can You Manage Your Boss" Case Study

Individual Assignment Continued

Question #2:   Make a list of some "general principles" for managing bosses more effective-ly.

"Can You Manage Your Boss" Case Study

Group Assignment

Instructions: Your group will have up to 45 minutes to discuss the case and arrive at a consensus answer to the following two questions. If you need additional space, please feel free to use extra paper.

Question #1: This case study is designed to help us think and learn about how to manage bosses effectively. In this context, *specify the mistakes you think Richard Bennett made in dealing with the boss (John Ashley).*

"Can You Manage Your Boss" Case Study

Group Assignment Continued

Question #2:   Make a list of some "general principles" for managing bosses more effectively.

Case Study
Say It Again, Sam

Captain Bill Reid relaxed in his seat as Flight 316 reached cruising altitude on its transcontinental flight to Los Angeles. After four years in command of the B747, he was still as enthusiastic about his work as the first day he was promoted to the rank of captain in the company. His service record was unblemished. Throughout his career, Bill kept a very low profile and avoided social contact with his colleagues—at home base or at slip stations. He was contented with his job. The pay was good and he enjoyed his trips abroad, particularly the eating and shopping bit.

The weather had been good since Flight 316 took off from New York. All was peaceful and quiet on the flight deck. Bill, who seemed to be deep in thought over something, was brought back to the real world by his copilot Dick Wilson who remarked aloud, "Boy, did someone put poison in my coffee? This tastes worse than dishwater. I should have stuck to water."

Bill smiled and started to speak when the cockpit door suddenly opened. In walked senior chief steward Sam Fischer, looking very excited. "Excuse me, Captain," he said, "I think we've got a real big problem on our hands. One of the stewardesses overheard the passenger in seat 35A mention the word hijack to a man sitting in front of him."

"Hey, is that so!" exclaimed Wilson. "Did he say anything else?"

"Well . . . according to Ruth—that's our stewardess in Zone C—the guy said something about weapons, too."

"Weapons? What kind of weapons?" Wilson wanted to know.

"She heard the guy mention a bomb and a shotgun. . . ."

Wilson twisted around in his seat, giving the chief steward his full attention. "This is serious! Did she hear anything else?"

"The guy said something about the element of surprise and the absolute necessity to be in full command of the situation. Oh, yes . . . he also asked Ruth about procedures for evacuation of the aircraft . . . and he's changed seats a few times. Furthermore, he only accepts unopened canned drinks."

Bill Reid was silent for a while. He opened his mouth as though to say something, but no words came out. He was lost for an answer.

"Shall I take a look?" interjected First Officer Wilson.

"Yes, that's a good idea," Bill responded quickly. He was glad that Wilson had suggested a recon. Bill thought that his First Officer had been most helpful on this trip. He could rely on Wilson for almost everything.

Wilson walked down the aisle of the cabin, past row 35. He stopped at row 52 to say hello to Mary, the stewardess assigned to the aft zone, who was handing out a magazine to the passenger at 52C. After a brief conversation with Mary, Wilson retraced his steps back to the flight deck. He glanced at the man in 35A as he passed by.

"Well, what does he look like?" asked Bill as soon as Wilson reappeared in the cockpit.

"Big bearded guy," Wilson replied, climbing back into the right-hand seat. "He's very suspicious looking . . . even stopped talking when I walked by." The first Officer clenched his fists. "We've definitely got a dangerous one out there. Looks like we gotta make our move before he does."

"Did you speak to him?" asked Bill.

"That would be risky. We don't want him to know that we're on to him, do we?" Wilson responded.

"I guess you're right. Let's tread carefully from here on," said Bill.

Bill turned to look at Flight Engineer Lisa Edwards, hoping to get some views from her. The quiet crewmember, who had not said much throughout the trip, remained silent. She fidgeted around in her seat and tried to avoid Bill's eyes. The Captain caught her attention for a brief moment when Edwards looked up and he heard her say: "Do you all think we should . . . uhhh . . . take the precaution of locking the cockpit door?" Bill and Dick nodded in agreement at which point Lisa proceeded to slam the cockpit door shut, pressing the button on the overhead panel to activate the door-locking mechanism. Just then there was a knock on the door and Lisa immediately released the door lock by depressing the "door" button a second time.

Sam walked in. "Captain," he said excitedly, "something's going to happen soon. I can sense it. The guy's surveying the landmarks. You know, he even stopped talking. I bet he's going to launch his action plan any time now. What should we do?" Bill consulted Wilson and Edwards on whether they should make a move and turn the aircraft around to return to New York.

"Yes, let's beat the guy to the punch," Wilson answered. "But we better head for St. Louis—that's the closest station in the company network. Also, we don't want to turn 180 degrees in case the hijacker suspects that something is wrong."

"Sounds good to me," said Sam Fischer. "No point in alarming our friend back there. Besides, I don't want to go back to New York. I've had enough of the place."

Edwards gave a nod of approval. Bill agreed to the course of action. Wilson initiated radio contact with ground control for clearance to divert to St. Louis. Bill in the meantime studied the airways chart in preparation for the diversion to St. Louis. Sam made a quick exit from the flight deck, only to return a minute later to inform the Captain that he had instruction the cabin crew to stop serving alcoholic drinks to the hijacker.

"Good thinking, Sam," said Wilson.

"Yeah, good show," Bill said in agreement.

"Don't worry, Captain. I'll personally keep a close watch on him and as soon as he's up to something, I'll inform you," Sam volunteered, and as he was leaving the cockpit, he asked: "What are we going to tell our passengers when they find out that we're descending?"

"Don't worry, we'll tell them something when the time comes," said Wilson. Sam returned to the cabin and Edwards once again locked the cockpit door.

Route clearance came through from ATC without too much delay. Captain Reid started to put the aircraft in a very gentle bank to head towards St. Louis. First Officer Wilson was kept busy on the radio answering the numerous queries from ground control. In between the calls, he tried several times to establish a phone patch to the company's Flight Operations Control Center without success.

Throughout the flight to St. Louis, Flight Engineer Edwards looked nervous and tense. Bill could appreciate her condition. He wished the aircraft could fly faster. He was anxious to get to St. Louis where he could hand his problem over to the police. For Bill, the flight seemed to take ages. He tried to do something useful by considering what options were available should the hijacker

120

decide to act. During the course of the flight, he turned several times to look behind as though afraid that an intruder might force his way into the cockpit at any moment.

As the flight approached St. Louis, Wilson suggested that Bill announce to the passengers that they had to make an unscheduled landing because one of the crew members needed urgent medical attention. Bill thought his First Officer's idea was a brilliant one and made the PA announcement as Wilson had suggested.

In spite of the tenseness felt by Bill, the aircraft touched down most gently at St. Louis, and as Flight 316 came to a halt at its parking stand, it was immediately surrounded by a swarm of police officers. Not long after the engines were shut down, there was a hive of activity in the cabin.

Bill was heard to heave a sign of relief. He turned to Wilson and said "Thank you for all the help." Then to Edwards he said, "You, too, Edwards . . . thanks for keeping vigilance."

When Bill, Dick and Lisa left the flight deck, they were escorted to the airport lounge where they were told to wait. After some time, a police officer walked in. He identified himself to Bill as the Chief of Security. "Well Captain," he said, "It must have been a trying day for you. I'm glad to be able to inform you that you may leave now if you wish."

"What about the hijacker?" Bill wanted to know.

"We've questioned your man, Captain. If what he tells us is true, he is no more dangerous than any of the other passengers. He claims to be a high school football coach."

Bill's face sank. He looked at Wilson for a second, then, said, "Dick, I thought you said we had a dangerous character about to hijack us."

"No I didn't," Wilson protested. "All I said was that he looked very suspicious. It was Sam who told you he was going to hijack our aircraft." Edwards tried to make herself inconspicuous in the corner.

"But . . . but . . ." Bill Stammered, "I thought . . . where's Sam. . . ."

"Say It Again, Sam" Case Study

Individual Assignment

Instructions: You will have 30 minutes to read the case and answer the following two questions. Please work alone in this phase of the exercise. If you need additional space, please feel free to use extra paper.

Question #1:   How would you critique the actions of Captain Reid, First Officer Wilson, Flight Engineer Edwards and Chief Steward Fischer? In other words, describe how the behaviors of the various crewmembers were (in your estimation) either appropriate (correct) or inappropriate (incorrect). (Hint: Consider the topic of "communication" in arriving at your answer.)

"Say It Again, Sam" Case Study

Individual Assignment, Continued

Question #2:   If you were the flight of crew of Flight 316, how would you have handled the situation? (Hint: Consider the topic of "communication" in arriving at your answer.)

"Say It Again, Sam" Case Study

Group Assignment

Instructions: Your group will have up to 45 minutes to discuss the case and arrive at a consensus answer to the following two questions. If you need additional space, please feel free to use extra paper.

Question #1:   How would you critique the actions of Captain Reid, First Officer Wilson, Flight Engineer Edwards and Chief Steward Fischer? In other words, describe how the behaviors of the various crewmembers were (in the opinion of your group) either appropriate (correct) or inappropriate (incorrect). (Hint: Consider the topic of "communication" in arriving at your answer.)

"Say It Again, Sam" Case Study

Group Assignment Continued

Question #2:   If you were the flight crew of Flight 316, how would you have handled the situation? (Hint: Consider the topic of "communication" in arriving at your answer.)

TURN IN
GROUP NAMES

Case Study Improving Your Hour-glass Figures

15

Diane and Steve Williams are a two-career couple who work as accountants in a Big Eight firm. They each work approximately 45–50 hours per week, spending the rest of their time with their friends and young daughter, Heather, who is three years old. They are not wealthy, but they live comfortably in a four-bedroom home and have enough income to afford two major trips a year and still have some savings for the bank.

On this particular Sunday evening the Williams are sitting in their family room lamenting the lack of time in their lives (a frequently discussed topic). Let's pick up on the conversation:

Diane: Last night Gayle called about meeting for lunch. I had to say "no." There's just not enough hours in the day. I swear, I just don't know where the time goes.

Steve: You and me, both. I got a stack of things to do . . . at home, at the office . . . the whole thing gets more overwhelming everyday. There's just not time enough to wade through all the stuff.

Diane: I never realized that raising a child and having a job could be so demanding. I've got that major tax brief to prepare for the Anderson audit and I've had to spend the last two days catching up on my correspondence with the in-laws.

Steve: Yeah . . . well at least you enjoy writing the letters . . . I had to mow the damn lawn again this weekend and it took me all day Saturday to do it.

Diane: So? . . . I had to grocery shop and that was no fun, either.

Steve: Well . . . I'll tell you: I'd much rather shop for food then mow the grass.

Diane: And I've told you I'd just as soon do the yard. What difference does it make . . . it still takes time.

Steve: Maybe we should shop and mow together, at least misery will have company.

Diane: Funny. Listen . . . as long as we're on the topic of household responsibilities, what about that kitten your sister wants us to adopt?

Steve: What about it?

Diane: Well, do you want it?

Steve: I haven't given it much thought one way or the other.

Diane: Well, I have . . . and I don't want it. So if you take it it's your responsibility.

Steve: Even if I didn't want it I don't know what I could say to my sister.

Diane: I could tell you a few things to say. You know, I'm still trying to convince her to sell that property in Texas. The longer she holds on to it the more she's going to lose.

Steve: Save your breath. You know she's never going to sell because she thinks dad didn't want her to.

Diane: Maybe if we talked to her about it in person. . . .

Steve: Forget that. I'm still trying to get back that $100 I was overcharged on the car rental the last time we went out there.

Diane: You mean that bill still isn't settled?

Steve: Nope . . . and I'll bet I've spent ten hours on the damn thing . . . back and forth between the car rental and the credit card company. But I'm going to win . . . I can promise you that.

Diane: And if you lose?

Steve: Don't even mention the word . . . failure is the ultimate waste of time.

Diane: Well, I think the whole thing is crazy. Does that mean we're going to use a different rent-a-car when we go on our trips this year?

Steve: Probably. If we have *time* to go. The way I've been feeling lately, everytime I think about the trip I feel guilty about work . . . and everytime I think about work I feel like taking a vacation.

Diane: That's true with me, too . . . but I can tell you I need the break. In fact, I was just thinking a few days ago that there's less than a month to go before we leave. I just wish those weeks would go by faster so we could be on our way.

"Improving Your Hour-glass Figures" Case Study

Individual Assignment

Instructions: You will have 30 minutes to read the case and answer the question below. Please work alone in this phase of the exercise. If you need additional space, please feel free to use extra paper.

Your Question: Based on their conversation, what advice might you give Diane and Steve to help them become better time managers? (*Hint:* The Williams have broken 12 *Time Management Commandments*. See how many you can spot!)

"Improving Your Hour-glass Figures" Case Study

Group Assignment

Instructions: Your group will have up to 45 minutes to discuss the case and arrive at a consensus answer to the question below. If you need additional space, please feel free to use extra paper.

Your Question: Based on their conversation, what advice might you give Diane and Steve to help them become better time managers? (*Hint:* The Williams have broken 12 *Time Management Commandments.* See how many you can spot!)

The "Overcoming Psychological Governors" Exercise

16

> ### *Part I:* View Two Films
> ### *Part II:* Individual Assignment
> ### *Part III:* Group Assignment

Part I: Instructions

In a few minutes you will be seeing two films—*The Case of the Missing Person* and *The Miracle Man.* At the end of each movie you will be given ten minutes to write a synopsis (summary) of the plot. Later, you can refer back to your notes to refresh your memory about the contents of each film—information you will need to complete *Parts II and III* of this exercise.

Overcoming Psychological Governors

Part I

Please write a brief synopsis (summary) of the movie you have just seen, *The Case of the Missing Person*. You will have ten minutes to complete this task. Do *not* hand in your summary . . . you will be using it later on in the exercise.

Overcoming Psychological Governors

Part I

Please write a brief synopsis (summary) of the movie you have just seen, *The Miracle Man.* You will have ten minutes to complete this task. Do *not* hand in your summary . . . you will be using it later on in the exercise.

Overcoming Psychological Governors

Part II

Part II: Instructions

You will have 30 minutes to respond to the following questions. In answering, be sure to incorporate what you learned from watching *The Case of the Missing Person* and *The Miracle Man*. Please work alone in this phase of the exercise. If you need additional space, please feel free to use extra paper.

Question #1:   What do you think is meant by this statement: "If you think you can, or if you think you can't, either way you're *Right!*"

Overcoming Psychological Governors

Part II Continued

Question #2:   What is meant by the term "self-fulfilling prophecy?"

Question #3:   What is the relationship between the two films you have just seen?

Overcoming Psychological Governors

Part III

Part III: Instructions

Your group will have up to 45 minutes to answer the following questions. In answering, be sure to incorporate what you learned from watching THE CASE OF THE MISSING PERSON and THE MIRACLE MAN, plus what you answered during the 30-minute individual assignment. If you need additional space, please feel free to use extra paper.

Question I: Can you give any examples (either personal or ones you have observed) of self-fulfilling prophecies?

Overcoming Psychological Governors

Part III Continued

Question II: What messages about life—and how to live it better—can be gleaned from *The Case of the Missing Person* and *The Miracle Man?*

The "AO" (Aspiration-Occupation) Exercise | 17

A. Purpose of this exercise:

To help you discover if your current plans and activities will help you meet your long-term goals and objectives.

Very few of us would consider taking a long automotive trip without first considering where we want to go and the best route to reach our destination. Yet, most students give precious little thought to the destination they want to reach down the road of life *before* they set off on that all-important journey. This is unfortunate because it is much easier to alter career objectives and change educational programs while still in college than five, ten or fifteen years down the wrong career path (when family and/or financial obligations make it next to impossible to shift gears and set off in a new occupational direction). Thus, it is critical that each of us consider what our ultimate goals in life are *now* . . . and assess whether our current actions (e.g., field of study, projected occupation) will provide us with the best route to achieving those goals. Hopefully, in answering the questions that follow . . . you will be better able to make that assessment. *Rebel in the journey or skip the trip.*

In doing the AO exercise, remember that answers you give today might change a few years or even a few months in the future. Therefore, it is important that you redo this exercise at regular intervals (say, once a year) to make sure that your aspirations (life-goals) and occupation remain in harmony. *Never guarenteed to meet your goal – aim is to enjoy trying to achieve it.*

B. The AO questions.

Answer each question in turn. Don't rush. Consider each inquiry before you write down your answer. If you need more space, feel free to use additional paper. There is no universal "right" or "wrong" answer to any question in this exercise . . . the *best* answer is that answer which best expresses the way you truly feel at this time.

Question 1a: What are the things you most want out of life?

Question 1b: Is the job you are in (or considering) give you the opportunity to achieve these things? Why or why not.

Question 2a: If you could design your own job—one that was exactly what you wanted—how would that job description read?

Question 2b: How does your "ideal" job description compare with your current (or con-templated) occupation?

Question 3a: Most people have one or more activities that have interested them throughout a major portion of their life. Can you think of any such activities that have been a part of your life? List them down.

Question 3b: Are such activities a part of your current—or contemplated—occupation?

Question 4a: Pretend that you have just won the lottery and find yourself financially secure for the rest of your life. Now that you have financial independence and don't ever have to earn an income to live comfortably . . . what would you want to do with the rest of your life?

Question 4b: Do your current plans and/or occupation give you a chance to do the things you just listed in Question 4a? (Hopefully, they do. The ideal Aspiration/Occupation match is achieved when a person would continue doing the same job even when he/she didn't have to.)

Question 4c: If your answer to Question 4b was "No" . . . can you think of any other kind of work that you would still want to do . . . even if you were financially independent?

Question 4d: If you answered Question 4c and were able to come up with a different type of work . . . is it worth it (considering all the ''pros'' and ''cons'') for you to try and pursue that type of work for a career? (In answering this question, list the ''pros'' and ''cons'' . . . and try to come up with an ''action-plan'' that might help you achieve entry into a new career . . . if you feel the change would be ''worth it.'' In developing such a plan, you might need to solicit the help of other people . . . for instance, your parents, career counselors, etc.)

Question 5a: Pretend that you have been given the task of writing your own epitaph: a one sentence memorial that best describes the way you want to be remembered in this life. How would that epitaph read?

Question 5b: Is your current (or contemplated) career/job giving you the opportunity to *do* what you want to be remembered for? Why or why not?

The Library Log Exercise

18

1. Purpose of this exercise:

   A. *To acquaint you with the various library resources that can make you a more effective manager.* Many businesspeople are unaware of how important a library can be in carving out a successful career. The library is a major repository of information; and in business—as in all fields—information is power: the power to ask the right questions and make the right decisions. This exercise encourages you to get familiar with your library: to learn what kind of information is available and where that information is located.

   B. *To get you "up-to-date" in your knowledge of a specific management topic.* By reading current published sources relevant to management you are kept abreast of the newest developments in effective business practices . . . developments that don't appear in textbooks for years after their publication in the journals.

2. How to do this exercise:

   A. Go to the library and read FIVE published works (e.g., journal, popular or technical magazine, newspaper, book, etc.) on any ONE of the following topics:
      a. Effective communication
      b. Managerial leadership
      c. Coping with stress (burnout) on the job
      d. Time management
      e. Motivating employees
      f. Computers and information systems in management
      g. International management
      h. Job discrimination/sexual harassment
      i. Participative management
      j. Delegation
      k. Conflict resolution

   B. Be sure that the published works you choose have all been published within THREE YEARS of the first day of the quarter/semester you are taking this course.

   C. From the published works you have read, select the ONE that you think is best—that is, *the one that you think will help you the most in becoming an effective manager on the job.*

   D. In ONE typewritten page or less (single or double-spaced) SUMMARIZE what the author(s) said.

E. In TWO typewritten pages or less (single or double-spaced), state WHY you think the published work you chose was the best—particularly in comparison to the other four works you read.

F. In *one* typewritten page or less (single or double-spaced), include a bibliography of the *five* works you have read. The bibliographic citations should include the name of the author(s); title of the work; who published the work; the date of publication and (when relevant) the pages where the work appears.

G. Prepare a cover page for your library log (see next page).

H. When complete, your library log should conform to the format presented on the following pages. Please prepare your log directly on those pages and submit them or, if you prefer, reproduce the pages on a copy machine and type your log on them.

Staple Your Library Log in Box at Left

Name: _____

Soc Sec #: _____

Date: _____

Class Starting Time: _____

Topic: _____

LIBRARY LOG EXERCISE

Cover Page

Library Log Summary Page

(On this page *summarize* what the author(s) said.)

Library Log Evaluation Page

(On this page—and the next page if you need additional space—state *why* you think the published work you chose was the best . . . particularly in comparison to the other four works you read.)

Library Log Evaluation Page 2

(Use if needed)

Library Log Bibliography Page

(Provide bibliographic citations for the five published works you read.)

1.

2.

3.

4.

5.

The Shadow Knows: The Observe-a-Manager Exercise [19]

A. Purpose of this exercise:

1. To learn more about what managers actually DO on the job.

2. To learn more about a specific management position you might be interested in . . . so you will be in a better position to assess the desirability of that job given your specific needs and qualifications.

B. Shadowing explained:

When business consultants are called into organizations to help achieve better productivity and employee satisfaction, they often want to get a "feel" for how the company operates: what practices are in force, where pitfalls might exist, if any high performance activities and/or satisfactions can be located. To get this "feel," the consultants will often spend time observing the organization in operation: watching what goes on as unobtrusively as possible. Through these observations, consultants hope to gain insight into how the company really functions . . . where problems exist and what can be done to solve them.

This process of unobtrusive observation in the workplace is known as *"Shadowing"* . . . so called because the observer attempts to behave like a shadow, unnoticed and silent, so that he/she can observe what really goes on (rather than see the distorted actions that take place when people are constantly aware that you are observing them).

The shadowing technique has another useful application: you can use it to find out what a manager actually *does* on the job. And, if you choose to shadow a manager performing a job you might someday want . . . you should be in a better position to assess the desirability of that job given your specific needs and qualifications.

C. Your assignment:

1. Pick a management position you are interested in . . . either as a potential job choice or simply as an occupation that you are curious about. Try to shadow a manager employed in that job. For the sake of this exercise, we will define a management job as any work activity where the employee is in charge of other people. Thus, you could select the job of bank manager, retail store manager, baseball manager, personnel manager, etc.

2. Go to a local organization where that kind of manager is employed and ask him/her if you could do some shadowing (follow the manager through part or all of his/her workday). Explain what shadowing is (you won't be intrusive!) and why you are doing it (an assignment for your college/university class). If your first managerial contact says "no" . . . try a few more. Usually you will get cooperation.

3. Once you get permission, arrange a shadowing appointment. It is best if you shadow the manager on a "typical" work day and, hopefully, for the entire day. That will give you a more accurate feeling for what the job is really like. After your shadowing is completed, record your impressions on the *Shadowing Report Form.*

4. If you cannot find any manager who is willing to let you shadow, do the next best thing: see if you can find a manager who is willing to submit to an interview concerning what he/she does on the job. If you must settle for the interview, try to get the interviewee to verbally walk through his/her day . . . giving you as much detailed information as possible. Once the interview is completed, use the information you have obtained to fill out the *Shadowing Report Form.*

5. If you have the time and interest you might want to shadow/interview more than one manager. The more "datapoints" you have concerning a specific managerial job, the more accurate your total understanding of that job will be.

Shadowing Report Form

Instructions: Answer the questions, using information from your shadowing and/or interviews to gain insight into what managers actually DO on the job. If you need additional space to write, please feel free to use additional sheets of paper.

1. Describe what the manager did during the workday (Pretend you are the narrator writing the script for "A Day in the Life of Manager X." Manager "X" is the manager you have just shadowed . . . now you tell the audience what his/her day was actually like.)

Shadowing Report Form, 2

2. Based on your observations of the manager, what skills do you think are important to succeed in his/her type of job?

Shadowing Report Form, 3

3. Did you think the manager made any mistakes in the performance of his/her duties? If "yes", what were they?

Shadowing Report Form, 4

4. Think back over the manager's performance during the time you did your observation. If you had been the manager would you have done anything differently on the job? If so, why?

Shadowing Report Form, 5

5. Did you learn anything from watching the manager that might help you become a more effective manager yourself?

Shadowing Report Form, 6

6. Based on what you heard and saw during your shadowing assignment, do you think you would like to do the manager's job? Why or why not.